ABOUT O'CASEY: The Playwright and the Work

Victoria Stewart studied English and Theatre Studies at the University of Sheffield and the University of Leeds and is now a Lecturer in the School of English, University of the West of England, Bristol.

Series Editor: Philip Roberts is Professor of Drama and Theatre Studies, and Director of the Workshop Theatre, at the University of Leeds. Educated at Oxford and Edinburgh, he held posts in the Universities of Newcastle and Sheffield before arriving in Leeds in 1998. His publications include: *Absalom and Achitophel and Other Poems* (Collins, 1973), *The Diary of Sir David Hamilton, 1709–1714* (Clarendon Press, 1975), *Edward Bond: A Companion to the Plays* (Theatre Quarterly Pubs., 1978), *Edward Bond: Theatre Poems and Songs* (Methuen, 1978), *Edward Bond: A Study of his Plays* (Methuen, 1980), *Bond on File* (Methuen, 1985), *The Royal Court Theatre, 1965–1972* (Routledge, 1986), *Plays without Wires* (Sheffield Academic Press, 1989), *The Royal Court Theatre and the Modern Stage* (CUP, 1999). In progress: *Taking Stock: the Theatre of Max Stafford-Clark* (to be published by Faber and Faber).

Associate Editor: Richard Boon is Professor of Performance Studies at the University of Leeds. He is the author of a number of studies of modern British political theatre, including *Brenton the Playwright* (Methuen, 1991), and is also co-editor of *Theatre Matters: Performance and Culture on the World Stage* (CUP, 1998).

in the same series

ABOUT BECKETT
The Playwright and the Work

ABOUT FRIEL
The Playwright and the Work

ABOUT HARE
The Playwright and the Work

ABOUT O'CASEY
The Playwright and the Work

Victoria Stewart

ff

faber and faber

First published in 2003
by Faber and Faber Limited
3 Queen Square London WC1N 3AU
Published in the United States by Faber and Faber Inc.
an affiliate of Farrar, Straus and Giroux LLC, New York

Typeset by Faber and Faber Limited
Printed in England by Bookmarque Ltd, Croydon

A CIP record for this book
is available from the British Library

ISBN 0-571-21059-8

2 4 6 8 10 9 7 5 3 1

Contents

Editors' Note

There are few theatre books which allow direct access to the playwright or to those whose business it is to translate the script into performance. These volumes aim to deal directly with the writer and with other theatre workers (directors, actors, designers and similar figures) who realize in performance the words on the page.

The subjects of the series are some of the most important and influential writers from post-war British and Irish theatre. Each volume contains an introduction which sets the work of the writer in the relevant historical, social and political context, followed by a digest of interviews and other material which allows the writer, in his own words, to trace his evolution as a dramatist. Some of this material is new, as is, in large part, the material especially gathered from the writers' collaborators and fellow theatre workers. The volumes conclude with annotated bibliographies. In all, we hope the books will provide a wealth of information in accessible form, and real insight into some of the major dramatists of our day.

Chronology of First Productions

Introduction

Sean O'Casey's writing career spanned a period of more than forty years, which included some of the most tumultuous times in the history of Ireland. He is still best known for the plays often referred to as the 'Dublin Trilogy', which deal with the human consequences of revolution and civil war, but he also produced plays notable for their use of expressionist and epic techniques, as well as a substantial autobiography, numerous essays, and poetry. This study aims to provide a sense of the scope and variety of O'Casey's work and thought throughout his writing career, and to indicate the range of influences that he drew on over the years, whilst also showing how a number of contemporary theatre practitioners have interpreted his plays.

In this introduction I will outline the social and political situation into which O'Casey was born and trace the path that led him to an association with Dublin's Abbey Theatre in the early 1920s. O'Casey's first play was not produced until he was in his early forties; lacking any substantial formal education, he made up for this through voracious reading and active participation in both political and theatrical groups. I will also explore the turns that his career took after he made the decision to leave Ireland for good in the late 1920s. During his time in England, he always remained concerned with Irish affairs and, as late as the 1950s, the controversy caused by his critique of the Catholic Church in his play *The Drums of Father Ned* (1958) led to him withdrawing his plays from professional performance in Ireland. This, as we shall see, was not the first time that one of his plays had proved to be controversial.

Beginnings: Ireland and Dublin in the late nineteenth century

O'Casey's father Michael Casey arrived in Dublin from the south-west of Ireland in the early 1860s, and in 1863 married Susan Archer, an auctioneer's daughter from Wicklow, to the south of Dublin. At this point, Ireland was still ruled from London, and had an economy based largely on agriculture. These two factors converged in the catastrophic famine of 1845–9, when the staple crop, the potato, was ravaged by blight, a fungal disease, and large numbers of the rural Irish died of illnesses related to malnutrition. Still debated by historians is the question of whether the government in London could have alleviated the situation more thoroughly and swiftly than it did; the famine is also credited with increasing the rate of emigration from Ireland. Many families left either for the United States or for large urban centres in England such as Liverpool. Relief for the poor during the hard times of the late 1840s was provided not only by the state but also by religious groups, including the Irish Church Mission, who, as David Krause has pointed out, offered both 'free soup and Protestant salvation'* to starving Catholics. It was for this organization that Michael Casey worked as a clerk, although there is no record of active religious campaigning on his part.

As Protestants in Dublin, the Casey family was part of a religious minority; at this time approximately eighty per cent of the city's population were Catholic. Although we cannot be sure, it is possible that O'Casey's parents had Anglo-Irish roots; the majority of Protestants had arrived in Ireland during earlier waves of immigration from England and Scotland. In the struggles for independence that were to gain momentum throughout the second half of the nineteenth century, a clear split was discernible between those in favour of establishing a government in Ireland and those who wished to stay united

* David Krause, *Sean O'Casey: The Man and His Work*, London: MacGibbon & Kee, 1960, p. 2.

with Britain. The former, the nationalists, were often Catholics, the latter, known as unionists, usually Protestant, with their political views reflecting their own ancestral roots. However, mapping these religious groups on to political affiliations in this general way should not obscure the fact that loyalties and allegiances were not always so straightforward and that nationalism, and the means by which it should be pursued, took different forms for different individuals. (We shall see that O'Casey was to become all too aware of the various splits and factions in the nationalist movement.) During his term as Prime Minister between 1868 and 1874, William Gladstone stated clearly that he wished to help calm these tensions: 'My mission is to pacify Ireland.'* There were attempts to facilitate a degree of self-rule for Ireland during this time, through the reform of laws to do with land ownership and the status of the Church of Ireland. After the defeat of Gladstone's government in the 1874 election, Home Rule was kept on the agenda by Irish politicians, notably Charles Stewart Parnell. It was also during this period of the late 1800s that various groups and societies concerned with the promotion of Irish national identity through art and culture began to increase in number and importance, and with these too Sean O'Casey was to have significant contacts.

Born John Casey on 30 March 1880 at the family home in North Dublin, the future playwright was the last of five children. That three other siblings did not survive infancy is a reflection of the high mortality rate in Dublin at the time, and O'Casey himself was seldom to enjoy good health. Although in 1885 he began attending St Mary's Infant School (where his sister Bella was a teacher), his education was seriously affected when he developed an ulcerated cornea. The treatment for this involved him spending large amounts of time either avoiding daylight or with his eyes actually bandaged, and his eyesight

---

* Quoted in Robert Kee, *The Green Flag: A History of Irish Nationalism*, London: Weidenfeld and Nicolson, 1972, p. 354.

was permanently damaged. This was the beginning of a condition that continued throughout his life, eventually leaving him almost completely blind. His attendance at school was only ever sporadic after this point. In his autobiographies, O'Casey describes having learned to read in his early teens, when he taught himself. Before this, he relied on his brothers to read aloud passages that he would then memorize. He later took pride in having been self-educated – he was often scornful of more formal educational methods – and it is evident that his admiration of Shakespeare, Dickens and other 'classics' was acquired through his own efforts.

When his youngest son was six, Michael Casey had a fall that caused fatal spinal injuries, and, with the main breadwinner gone, the family often had a difficult time making ends meet. During O'Casey's childhood they were obliged to move house a number of times to less expensive accommodation, and in 1894, at the age of fourteen, O'Casey went out to work for the first time, as a warehouse man. The following year, his brother Archie, who had long been involved in amateur dramatics, helped him to his first stage role, that of the honest and kind-hearted Father Dolan in Dion Boucicault's *The Shaughraun* (1874). Boucicault was the leading Irish exponent of the popular nineteenth-century dramatic form, the melodrama, and the plot of *The Shaughraun* contained many of melodrama's typical ingredients: a struggle between the virtuous lower classes and a cruel property owner, romantic entanglements, and elaborate demands on staging (at one point a character is required to jump off the edge of a cliff into the sea). The use of minor characters to provide comic relief, and the class-based struggle at the heart of the play can be seen to foreshadow O'Casey's Dublin plays, although any melodramatic elements in a play such as *Juno and the Paycock* are tempered by its realism in both setting and language. Coincidentally, the performance of *The Shaughraun* in which O'Casey performed took place at the Mechanics Theatre, later to become the home of the Abbey Theatre Company. During this time, as O'Casey later told his

4

interviewers, he was also beginning to attend the theatre, developing his interest in Shakespeare and other playwrights. At work, however, things were not progressing smoothly. O'Casey was sacked from his first job in 1897, and the following year was dismissed after only a week at a wholesale newsagents for refusing to remove his cap when receiving his wages.

Religion was still an important part of his life at this time; O'Casey had been confirmed into the Church of Ireland in 1898 and between 1900 and 1903 he taught in a Sunday School. It was also during this period that he became involved not only in the increasingly popular Irish nationalist associations but also in the labour movement. Both these types of societies were important in shaping his future attitude towards Irish independence. He joined the Gaelic League, which had been founded in 1893 by Douglas Hyde and Eoin Mac Neill for the promotion of Irish language and culture, and also the Gaelic Athletic Association, founded in 1884, which organized Gaelic sports, such as hurling. In the spirit of these organizations and in common with many others, he 'Gaelicized' his name and became Sean O'Cathasaigh, altering this to O'Casey when his first play was produced by the Abbey, and also began to teach himself the Irish language. These societies were not explicitly political in intent and did not campaign in an overt way for political reform, except by the indirect (but nonetheless significant) route of demanding bilingual road signs and the introduction of compulsory Irish in schools. They did foster an interest in the creation of a specifically Irish identity and history, and this aim was shared by the poet W. B. Yeats and by Lady Gregory, who, at the turn of the century and together with the playwright J. M. Synge, founded the Irish National Theatre Society. Yeats and Gregory were particularly interested in exploring Irish mythology and history. In Yeats's play *Cathleen ni Houlihan* (1902), for example, an old woman arrives at a cottage on the coast and tells the inhabitants that she has had her four fields stolen from her, that there are strangers in her house and that many men have died for her.

At the climax of the play the inhabitants of the cottage see troops landing nearby. The woman leaves, but those who pass her in the road see not an old woman but a beautiful young girl. The historical reference point here is the rebellion of 1798, which was spearheaded by the nationalist United Irishmen; the character of Michael in the play, who is about to be married, falls under the spell of the old woman's patriotic rhetoric. He follows her when she leaves, indicating his intention to help this embodiment of Ireland to recoup her losses. The idealized and often sentimental nature of such representations of the Irish struggle did not escape notice, especially after the events of 1916, and this mythical vision of rural Ireland was certainly far from any of O'Casey's early experiences.

If his involvement with the Gaelic organizations reflected his continuing drive to educate himself, O'Casey's involvement in labour movements was partly provoked by his starting work as a labourer on the railways in 1902. He was forced to leave his job in 1911 when he refused to sign an undertaking not to join the Irish Transport and General Workers Union (ITGWU), which had been formed by Jim Larkin, who was to be an influential figure for O'Casey in his championing of workers' rights. The 1911 strike of railway workers figured in O'Casey's later writing, including *The Star Turns Red* (1940), where the main character, 'Red Jim', struggles with the demands of the Church, the state and his union. As his own involvement in the union movement grew, O'Casey's religious interests dwindled; his commitments were now to nationalist and workers' associations. Since 1902 he had been a member of the Irish Republican Brotherhood (IRB), also known as the Fenians, which since its formation in 1858 as a secret society had become established as a voice of republican separatism. However, his belief not only in workers' rights but also in Irish nationalism was to lead him to resign from both the IRB and the Gaelic League in 1912 over what he considered to be their lack of concern for labour issues and the conditions of the workforce. He was interested only in a workers' republic, not in one that would only be advantageous for the elite, and he began to contribute to the *Irish Worker*, a union newspaper, and *Irish Freedom*, a nationalist journal.

Union-related unrest was growing in Dublin: in early 1913 the Dublin United Tramways Company refused to employ members of the ITGWU and locked the workers out, sparking strikes and violent unrest. O'Casey became secretary of the Strike Relief Fund. The dispute continued for some months, with support dwindling only as winter set in. In response to police attacks on demonstrators, in November 1913 the union instituted the Irish Citizen Army (ICA) in an attempt at self-defence. Towards the end of the year another paramilitary organization, the Irish Volunteers, was formed, and with the outbreak of the First World War, splits and reaffiliations occurred among these groups that were to have important effects on O'Casey's future involvement with them. The Irish Volunteers divided into two factions: the majority supported John Redmond, the leader of the Irish Parliamentary Party, and wanted to join in the war against Germany, whilst the rest, a group that had been influenced by the IRB, wanted to join with the ICA and prepare for revolt against Britain. A particular bone of contention for O'Casey was the position of Countess Markievicz (born Constance Gore-Booth and married to a member of the Polish aristocracy), who was a member of both the Volunteers and the ICA, and who urged that the groups should be merged. For O'Casey, this would have meant the triumph of the kind of nationalism that had led him to leave the IRB in the first place, a movement that would not give the workers their full due. O'Casey presented a motion demanding that Markievicz choose between the two organizations, but this was defeated by a single vote. He resigned from the ICA, his disaffection increasing when James Connolly took over its leadership after Larkin went to the United States on a fundraising trip.

O'Casey's increasing distance from the ICA meant that he took no active part in the 1916 Easter Rising, which was instigated by the ICA, IRB and the Volunteers. The events began with the occupation of Dublin General Post Office and led to running battles in the streets. Patrick Pearse, the Director of Military Operations for the IRB, who delivered the Proclamation of Independence during the occupation of the GPO, had himself come to support the active nationalist movement after developing a passionate belief in the importance of the Irish language, and was prominent in the Gaelic League. However, it is not merely for their belief in the idea of Ireland that those involved in the events of 1916 came to be seen as martyrs in republican circles. Military assistance from abroad failed to materialize, British troops were sent in, and fourteen key figures in the rebellion, including Pearse and Connolly, were taken to Kilmainham Jail, found guilty of treason, and faced death by firing squad.

These events were to form the background to *The Plough and the Stars* (1926), which offers a critique of the Easter Rising and its legacy. (The speech delivered by the Figure in the Window in Act Two is an edited version of Pearse's Proclamation of Independence.) I will return later to the furore that greeted this play when it was first staged; but it is also worth noting that the aftermath of the rising was the occasion for a prose work by O'Casey, *The Sacrifice of Thomas Ashe* (1918). Ashe was known to O'Casey through his association with the Gaelic League and the Volunteers. He was arrested in 1917 on suspicion of involvement in political activity and organized a hunger strike in Dublin's Mountjoy Prison, as a protest against the treatment of political prisoners. He died in prison in September 1917 after having been force-fed and tortured, and O'Casey's short book is an emotive memorial to Ashe's bravery. O'Casey also published *The Story of the Irish Citizen Army* in 1919. Although this was an official history of the movement, he made clear his own feelings about the path that the organization had taken. From this point on, and as political and military unrest continued in Ireland, his writings, although still expressive of political concerns, were driven predominantly by literary considerations.

Becoming a playwright

O'Casey first visited the Abbey Theatre, the home of the Irish National Theatre Society, in 1917, for a production of Oliver St John Gogarty's play *Blight: The Tragedy of Dublin*. Gogarty is now better known as a poet and for his autobiography *As I Was Going Down Sackville Street* (1936), and this was his only full-length play. It is not difficult to see why it would have interested O'Casey. Set in the Dublin tenements, it highlights the inadequacy of charitable work as a means of dealing with the problems of slum-dwellers. The main character in the play, Stanislaus Tully, has been injured at work and is exaggerating the seriousness of his problem in order to be able to claim compensation. When he receives £300 in this dishonest way, he decides to become a landlord himself. Echoes of this plot were to feature in O'Casey's later work – tenement dwellers coming into money form the focal point of *Juno and the Paycock* – but perhaps most notable are the connections between Stanislaus Tully and the character of Captain Boyle in *Juno*. As important as any explicit likeness between these characters, who are both work-shy drinkers who spend a proportion of their time dodging debt collectors, is the fact that, as O'Casey made clear to many of his interviewers, this was a milieu with which he was very familiar. Like Gogarty, he wished to expose and explore the experiences of people living in such conditions, although in O'Casey's early works there was to be less satire and more sympathy.

The Abbey had been founded with the express intention of presenting plays exploring specifically Irish themes and ideas, whether these be represented in a realistic fashion, as in a play like Gogarty's, or in a more symbolic way, as in Yeats's work. It also had a reputation for staging works of a controversial nature; Synge's *Playboy of the Western World* had provoked riots in 1907 because of its earthy and, some felt, offensive portrayal of Irish peasant life. Audience disquiet came to a head with Christy Mahon's line towards the end of the play,

'. . . what'd I care if you brought me a drift of chosen females, standing in their shifts itself maybe . . .' – a shift being an item of women's underwear. The whole thrust of the play seemed to be demanding self-reflection and, implicitly, self-criticism on the part of the more idealistic nationalists, demands that were to be reiterated, albeit in a very different social context, in O'Casey's work. In 1920, O'Casey submitted two plays for consideration *The Harvest Festival*, and *The Frost and the Flower*. *The Harvest Festival* had been rejected by the social club for which he originally wrote it, as it was felt to be based rather too closely on the lives of other group members.* These two plays were rejected by the Abbey, but in 1922 *On the Run*, later rewritten and renamed *The Shadow of a Gunman*, was accepted. The play had been inspired by the Royal Irish Constabulary's midnight raids on the house in Mountjoy Square where O'Casey was sharing a flat (he had moved there following his mother's death in 1919). The play was staged for a brief run in 1923, and proved popular. Later the same year a one-act piece by O'Casey, *Kathleen Listens In*, was staged as part of a triple bill with Lady Gregory's *The Rising of the Moon* and George Bernard Shaw's *The Man of Destiny*.

During the early 1920s, the future political make-up of Ireland was being decided. Following the Easter Rising the different aims and objectives of the various factions in the republican movement, and the fact that unionism, particularly concentrated in the north-east of Ireland, was also a force to be reckoned with, led to a continuation of violence. The Government of Ireland Act (1920) proposed the partition of the country into Northern Ireland, comprising six counties of Ulster, and Southern Ireland, known from 1922 as the Irish Free State. The War of Independence, which had begun in 1919, was halted by a truce in July 1921, and concluded by a

---

* *The Frost and the Flower* is now lost; *The Harvest Festival* was discovered after O'Casey's death and eventually published in 1979, but it has never been performed.

treaty in December that year, after negotiations between the British government and an Irish delegation led by Arthur Griffith and Michael Collins. Although narrowly passed by the Irish Parliament, this treaty was seen as an unacceptable compromise by republicans. The civil war, fought between pro-treaty and anti-treaty forces, lasted from spring 1922 to summer 1923 and ended in defeat for the anti-treaty republicans. During the run of *Shadow of a Gunman*, the Abbey was under threat from the IRA, which had ordered the closure of theatres as a protest against the treaty. Yeats was a senator in the new Free State government, which increased the likelihood of the theatre coming under attack. It is perhaps not surprising in these circumstances that, as Christopher Murray has noted, the first audiences for the play 'preferred to ignore the tragic side'* of the play and focus on the satire.

The events of the civil war formed the background to *Juno and the Paycock*, staged by the Abbey in 1924. The down-to-earth portrayal of tenement dwellers in this play caused some disquiet among more idealistic audience members; this, however, was nothing in comparison with the outrage provoked by *The Plough and the Stars* when it was presented the following year. The outcry over this play was compared to that which *The Playboy of the Western World* had prompted. Yeats, as in the earlier instance, took the opportunity to berate the audience for its lack of understanding of the play's intentions. Once again nationalist sentiments were offended. O'Casey took part in a public debate about the play with Hannah Sheehy-Skeffington. She was the widow of Francis Sheehy-Skeffington, whose death had been one of the outrages of the Easter Rising. Having taken a stand against the use of violence by resigning from the ICA when it had become an armed force, he was shot in 1916 by a British soldier after being captured while trying to prevent looting. Hannah Sheehy-Skeffington's complaint against the play was that O'Casey was besmirching the mem-

* Christopher Murray, *Sean O'Casey*, London: Faber and Faber, 2001, p. 45.

ory of those days by not only showing the heroes of the rebellion in a public house, but also having them bring with them the flag of the play's title. The inclusion of the character of Rosie the prostitute was also deemed offensive. For O'Casey, his critics were simply denying the reality that he could see all around him.

The reaction to *The Plough and the Stars* was not the only reason for O'Casey deciding to extend his 1926 visit to London into a permanent residence in England. Tensions had been growing between him and various figures at the Abbey, but the events surrounding the denunciation of *The Plough and the Stars* must also have seemed to O'Casey to be a manifestation of the kind of nationalism he had wished to avoid. O'Casey initially went to London to receive the Hawthornden Literary Prize for *Juno and the Paycock*, but a production of *The Plough and the Stars* was also under way. Cast in the role of Nora as a last minute replacement was a young Irish-born actress, Eileen Carey. The following year, with O'Casey installed in a flat in London, they married. During this time O'Casey was working on *The Silver Tassie*, which he duly submitted to the Abbey. This play deals with the First World War and its impact on a group of young men and their families, and is striking in its use of expressionist techniques, particularly in its second act. This takes place on a stylized battlefield, and the characters speak for the most part in verse, while the mysterious Croucher acts as a chorus. Although the subject matter – the effects of war and violence – was familiar, O'Casey was beginning the experiments with form and style that would be characteristic of his later writings. However, by an unfortunate coincidence, he received a letter of rejection from the Abbey on the day of his son Breon's birth. Despite his own interest in experimental and non-realistic dramatic forms, W. B. Yeats felt that the play was not successful. He also suggested that O'Casey had insufficient emotional investment in the course of the First World War, and that his earlier plays had had greater impact because they dealt with Irish issues closer to his heart: 'You were interested in the

Irish Civil War, and at every moment of those plays wrote out of your own amusement with life or your sense of its tragedy . . . But you are not interested in the Great War; you never stood on its battlefields or walked its hospitals, and so write out of your opinions.'* With George Bernard Shaw on his side, O'Casey withdrew the play from the Abbey and a production was mounted in London. The Abbey did eventually stage *The Silver Tassie* in 1935, by which time O'Casey had made peace with Yeats, but he was to retain a suspicion of any establishment, be it theatrical or indeed religious, that seemed to be preventing freedom of expression.

'Exile' in England

In later years, O'Casey's decision to settle in England was sometimes interpreted as an anti-Irish gesture; O'Casey's response to this would usually be to draw a distinction between the people of Ireland and those who ruled the country. The family moved to Buckinghamshire in 1931, and Eileen continued to take acting roles, but it was often difficult to make ends meet. In 1932 O'Casey sold the amateur rights for his plays for £300; the need for ready cash meant that he would forgo the not inconsiderable sum that would otherwise have come to him from this source over the years. In 1934 he published *Within the Gates*, a play drawing on his experiences of visiting Speakers' Corner, in Hyde Park, London, the traditional gathering point for those keen to preach on politics, religion, or indeed their own eccentricities. As O'Casey indicates in an interview from 1927 (see pp. 28–9), he was enthralled by the speakers he witnessed there. He travelled to see *Within the Gates* produced in the United States, and it was during this trip that he encountered the American playwright Eugene O'Neill. O'Neill, who had already been awarded the Pulitzer Prize for

---

* *The Letters of W. B. Yeats*, ed. Allan Wade, London: Rupert Hart-Davis, 1954, pp. 740–41.

Anna Christie (1921) and *Strange Interlude* (1928), was to receive the Nobel Prize for Literature in 1936, and O'Casey remained an admirer of O'Neill's work throughout his life. The combination of realistic emotional insight and techniques such as symbolic stage settings and the use of characters who perform the function of a chorus were common to the work of both playwrights. O'Casey never used autobiographical material in his drama as extensively as O'Neill did, but during the 1930s O'Casey did begin work on an autobiography that was to grow into his most substantial piece of non-dramatic writing. O'Casey's second son Niall was born in 1935, and his daughter Shivaun four years later, by which time the family had moved on to Totnes, in Devon, where O'Casey was to live for the rest of his life. The first of his six volumes of autobiographical writings, *I Knock at the Door*, which deals with the hardships of his childhood, was published in 1939, and was promptly banned in Ireland because of the frankness with which it deals with adolescent experiences of sexuality. (This ban was eventually lifted in 1947.) Successive volumes were to appear through the 1940s, with the final one, *Sunset and Evening Star*, appearing in 1954. In all these, O'Casey writes about himself in the third person as 'Johnny Casside'. This narrative technique gives him the freedom to slip inside characters' heads and describe their personal feelings, whilst also maintaining a degree of artistic distance from the events recounted.

Although O'Casey's days as a labourer were by now remote, they were not forgotten, and his continuing concern with labour issues was reflected in his other writing of the thirties and forties. *The Star Turns Red*, written in 1938–9 and first performed in 1940, deals with a workers' uprising, and during the war years O'Casey not only became a member of the editorial board of the communist newspaper the *Daily Worker* but also, as I have noted, returned to the 1911 rail strike in *Red Roses for Me* (1943). *Purple Dust*, a satire on the pretensions of the English upper-middle classes and their sentimental attitudes to Ireland, was also staged in 1943, and O'Casey tackled the Second World War itself, specifically the Battle of Britain and the Soviet Union's joining with the Allies, in *Oak Leaves and Lavender* (1946). The play that he later described as his favourite of his own works, *Cock-a-Doodle Dandy*, appeared in 1949.

In the post-war years O'Casey was also writing essays on political and theatrical themes, and some of these appeared in 1956 as *The Green Crow*. Like many of his previous writings, this volume was temporarily banned in Ireland and his difficult relations with that country were far from over. In 1955 the Gaiety Theatre's production of *The Bishop's Bonfire*, a satire on the Catholic Church, was preceded by vicious attacks on O'Casey in the Catholic press. The production itself passed without incident. Next, however, O'Casey's *The Drums of Father Ned* was chosen to be included in the 1958 Tostal, an annual festival of Irish culture established not long before by the Irish Tourist Board. Also to be performed was an adaptation of James Joyce's *Ulysses*. The Archbishop of Dublin refused to mark the opening of the Tostal with a mass if these plays were included, and both were removed from the programme. O'Casey was furious, and banned professional productions of his plays in Ireland. The expression of anti-Catholicism to be found in these works can, of course, be seen as part of a larger set of concerns that emerged throughout O'Casey's life; he saw the Church as yet another force that prevented Ireland from achieving the kinds of political reforms that had so interested and fired him over the years.

In his final years O'Casey continued to write short plays including *The Moon Shines on Kylenamoe* and *Figuro in the Night* (both 1959). His final full-length play, *Behind the Green Curtains*, was also written in 1959, and publication of his essays continued, with *Under a Colored Cap* appearing in 1963. The ban on Irish productions of his plays was lifted when the Abbey company was invited to take part in a season in London in 1964 commemorating the four-hundredth anniversary of Shakespeare's death, and O'Casey allowed *The Plough and the Stars* and *Juno and the Paycock* to be performed. On 18 September that year, at the age of eighty-four, he died of a heart attack.

O'Casey's legacy

It is tempting to divide Sean O'Casey's writing career neatly into two parts: the realistic, historically engaged Dublin plays, and the later, more abstract works written after his move to England, with *The Silver Tassie* bridging the gap between. The later plays do move away from the strictly realistic settings and action of the earlier ones, but it is worth considering both the contextual reasons why this might be the case, and the ways in which O'Casey can be seen to develop particular themes and interests throughout his writing career.

As I have indicated, the influences on O'Casey's early writing were various. The playwrights who emerged from the Abbey in the early years of the century cannot be said to form a 'school' as such, as although they were all concerned with specifically Irish issues, their stylistic approaches varied greatly, from the melodrama of a writer like Gogarty, to the symbolism of Yeats. The plays of the 'Dublin Trilogy' also have a strong strand of humour, often focused on male 'double acts', such as Joxer Daly and Captain Boyle in *Juno and the Paycock*, and can therefore be described as 'tragicomedy', this mixed genre reflecting the variety of influences that feed into them. After the move to England, and particularly after settling in Devon, O'Casey was no longer a regular theatre-goer, although, as the interviews collected here reveal, he continued to read widely. The lack of access to performers who could test out his work in progress might lead to a suggestion that the later plays are best considered as chamber dramas, to be read rather than performed; but in fact plays such as *Cock-a-Doodle Dandy* and *Purple Dust* pose real theatrical challenges that demand practical solutions. There are also thematic links that connect the later to the earlier plays. The comic elements recur and, in a play like *Cock-a-Doodle Dandy*, take on an element of the carnivalesque. Comedy is celebrated for its disruptive potential, and the power it has to expose the hypocrisies of everyday life. O'Casey celebrates the power of women in a similar way. If Juno can be seen as in some respects representative of the particular burden that women have to bear in times of revolution and war, Loreleen in *Cock-a-Doodle Dandy* stands for freedom from hypocrisy and hope for the future, even though this is expressed in less specifically political terms.

O'Casey remained an eclectic writer and also retained an interest throughout his life in current developments in theatre. In 1950, for example, he participated in a debate in the pages of the *New Statesman and Nation* that had been begun by Terence Rattigan. Rattigan, a playwright known for light comedies and dramas, suggested that plays should deal with relationships between people, rather than ideas. One of his prime targets was George Bernard Shaw, an ally of O'Casey's from the occasion when Yeats rejected *The Silver Tassie*. O'Casey lost little time in writing to defend Shaw and to reinforce his belief in the power of drama to affect individuals both personally and politically, harking back to his days as a labourer and remembering the influence that reading Shaw and Shakespeare had had on his own political development. He summed up his argument: 'A new kind of life is with us, whether we like it or not . . . The plays written around the new life must be in the mainstream of drama, must be an offspring of the great tradition . . . I look forward to the day with confidence when British workers will carry in their hip pockets a volume of Keats's poems or a Shakespeare play.'[*] Towards the very end of his life, O'Casey attacked the latest wave of new playwrights, many of whom showed the influence of absurdism, suggesting that they were overly pessimistic. In his final essay, 'The Bald Primaqueera' (the title a reference to Eugene Ionesco's 1950 play, *The Bald Prima Donna*) he expressed a dislike for the

---

[*] 'The Play of Ideas' (1950), reprinted in *Blasts and Benedictions*, selected and introduced by Ronald Ayling, London: Macmillan, 1967, pp. 24–6 (p. 26).

works of Harold Pinter, whom he described as 'a sinister fellow as far as his work is concerned'.* More to his taste was John Arden's use of an epic style in *Serjeant Musgrave's Dance* (1960). As the interviews collected here show, O'Casey always retained a faith in the positive effects his drama could have on audiences, and the combination of qualities that he ascribed to Arden – 'power, protest and frantic compassion'† – is an equally good summation of his own work.

* 'The Bald Primaqueera' (1964), reprinted in *Blasts and Benedictions*, pp. 63–76 (p. 70).
† 'The Bald Primaqueera', (p. 74).

2

Interviews with 'Outsiders'

The interviews chosen for this book span the whole of O'Casey's career. The earliest interviewers tend to focus on the 'rags to riches' (or at least 'building site to playwright') aspect of O'Casey's story, but after his move to England interviewers are more inclined to discuss the details of his work and political opinions. There are relatively few interviews from the period 1935–50, partly because at this time O'Casey's main writing project was his autobiography, which put him into the public eye only sporadically. The interviews from the later period illustrate the extent of O'Casey's international reputation and his eagerness to express his views on current affairs as well as on specifically theatrical matters.

'The Author of *Juno*: A Talk with Mr O'Casey', by 'A Correspondent', *Observer*, 22 November 1925

I knocked at a door in the hall of a high tenement house in Dublin. A man in his shirt-sleeves answered. The man was Sean O'Casey, whose play *Juno and the Paycock* is now at the Royalty Theatre, London.

As he finished dressing in the darkness of the room where he lives, works, and sleeps, cooking for himself as he did when a brick-setter's labourer, two years ago, he talked in his soft Dublin tongue, using the speech of a writer and the accent of a workman. 'Born in a tenement house, I write about people in tenement houses,' he told me. 'If the London production is a success, I'll leave 'em for ever.'

Mr O'Casey is forty-one, is frank, unaffected, likeable, and (so he says) lazy. A slim, hatchet-faced man, with pointed nose and chin, and brown, twinkling weak eyes, so weak, I believe, that he has to hold his manuscript six inches or so from his nose to read what he has written. He works at all hours when the mood and the idea are there. 'I make no division of day and night,' he said. He writes in copybooks, leaving the play loose and flexible, and then types it out twice, altering, altering. 'It would not be true, perhaps, to say that the first draft bears no resemblance to the finished play, but they are very different.'

I spoke to him of technique. 'I abominate it,' he said. 'They tell me *The Shadow of a Gunman* breaks all the rules. If the characters live and the play holds the audience, that's enough.'

Mr O'Casey has had a hard life. He told me his father died when he was three, and that his mother brought the family up. 'We had dry bread and a drink of tea in the morning, and that again at night if we were lucky.' For nine years, he half-starved. At fourteen he taught himself to read: at fifteen he worked for a newsagent from 4 a.m. to 7 p.m. for 9s. a week. After that he navvied and laboured for fifteen years. His last job, oddly enough, was on a building near the Abbey Theatre, which he has visited for the past ten years, and into which he drops nearly every evening.

He has views on education. 'Education is a terrible drawback to a dramatist – I mean the sort of primary and secondary education we get in Ireland. You can see from the way my plays are written I never went to school.' He said that quite seriously. 'The first book I bought was Shakespeare. I spent nearly all my money on books.'

I mentioned the criticism that has been made that his plays are a series of photographs, and that he writes only of what he knows, of his own experiences. 'What in the name of heaven should a man write about?' he asked. 'What did Euripides and Aristophanes write about? My next play will be *The Red Lily* – about a prostitute. I wonder if that will suit them? I worked with Captain Boyle, a character in *Juno*, for five years. I didn't even alter his name. No, I don't think he ever saw the play.'

On the subject of acting he said he had acted a little in an amateur way. 'But I go to all the rehearsals in the Abbey, and I sometimes act the characters for them there.'

Mr O'Casey wrote three plays – one two-act and two three-act – before *The Shadow of a Gunman* was accepted in 1923. Since then he has written *Juno and the Paycock*, *Nannie's Night Out* (one-act), and *The Plough and the Stars*, which he has just completed. Lady Gregory, Mr Yeats, and Mr Lennox Robinson* think highly of *The Plough*, he told me. It will be done at the Abbey Theatre within a few weeks. 'The output isn't bad,' said Mr O'Casey, 'but I'm afraid I'm very lazy.' Of the future, he declared, 'One never knows what one will write, but I'll never write a novel. I don't like novels. But plays! I think writing plays, bringing people to life – that is charming work. I wouldn't change that for anything.'

'Sean O'Casey sees London: Irish Dramatist's First Visit to England', *Evening Standard*, 5 March 1926

Sean O'Casey, the remarkable Irish playwright, who until six weeks ago was a labourer, has arrived in London for the first time in his life. He has never before crossed the Irish Channel, and he has come here expressly to see his play *Juno and the Paycock*, when it is transferred to the Royalty Theatre from the Fortune on Monday.

'My first impression of London has been one of sleeplessness,' he told an *Evening Standard* representative today. 'I am not accustomed to a big hotel, and everything was so quiet last night that I listened for the familiar noises of the tenement quarter in which I live in Dublin. An author abroad should live in the atmosphere of the places and people about whom he writes. Then only can he hope to get a true perspective. Thus I wrote about people of tenement regions, and I lived, and still live, in a single room in a quarter like to that I have tried to describe.

* Lennox Robinson (1886–1958), an actor and director, was associated with the Abbey from its foundation.

'Whatever literary attainments I have came from a desire for knowledge. The trouble with our modern system is, as it seems to me, that we study too much. Education suffers from too much study. What is more important is a true perception of the relation of learning (a hateful word) with art and literature.

'Modern civilisation must learn that all intelligence does not belong to the middle or upper classes. The working classes have their share, and I think the time will come when everybody, son of a cook, son of a millionaire, will go to the same schools . . .

'Reading Shakespeare did not make me a playwright. That came about in this way. I was a member of a Gaelic or national club, which had for its original object the teaching of Irish and the encouragement of the hurley game. One day they decided to produce a play, but because they had no money the plays they tackled were very uninteresting.

'By this time I could write a little, and I was presumptuous enough to suggest that I wrote a play myself. It was a poor two-act affair called *The Frost and the Flower*, but because it reflected on the family life of two or three members it was rejected, and I sent it to the Abbey Theatre, where it remained for six months before it was returned with an encouraging letter. This stimulated me to write another play, called *The Harvest Festival*. It suffered the same fate, and I wrote another, *The Crimson and the Tricolour*, a Labour play, which my friends at the Abbey kept for twelve months, decided to produce, and then, at the last minute, returned.

'Twelve months is a long time, and I had employed it in writing another piece, called *The Shadow of a Gunman*, and this they produced at last in 1923. I was elated, and began to write phantasies on politics. One of these, *Kathleen Listens In*, was done at the Abbey, but it was so badly received that I went home almost broken-hearted, without going behind even to thank the artists. And that same night in my attic I sat down to write *Juno and the Paycock*, and here I am in London fulfilling an ambition of mine.'

'Sean O'Casey's Pawned Trousers', by 'Mr Gossip', *Daily Sketch*, 6 March 1926.

I had a chat with Sean O'Casey in a quiet cafe yesterday with Mr and Mrs J. B. Fagan. A slight, almost insignificant-looking man until one catches his small penetrating eyes, he has no false estimation of his position as an artist or man of the world, and until we talked of the miserable wages of the labourer he was complacent as a dove.

'Three weeks before *Juno and the Paycock* was produced,' he said, 'I pawned my trousers for five shillings and earned wages insufficient for the nourishment of a dog. What's the use of singing "The Red Flag" when men will accept 30s. for a week's hard labour?'

Incidentally Sean O'Casey said he thought his next play would wreck the Abbey Theatre. Talking of English playwrights, he said they did not appeal to him. Galsworthy had enormous power and conviction, but his style was, perhaps, a little too polished and in danger of being untrue to life. 'The Irishman,' he went on, 'hasn't any sentimentality. He behaves when he is drunk as an Englishman does when he is sentimental.'

While we talked someone walked in and nearly roused O'Casey to anger.

'I suppose,' he said, 'that when you have made a lot of money you'll move among the best people in Dublin.'

O'Casey blew a cloud of smoke.

'Tell me,' he replied, 'do your best people live in tiled bathrooms or floorless barns?

'I shall continue to live in my room where I have always worked . . . There is a fine fellowship with those among whom I lived minus a shirt for months. I like London, but I don't understand the English. What did that waitress say? The bill? That should have been obvious enough.'

'O'Casey Explains Himself', by Constance Vaughan, *Daily Sketch*, 24 March 1926.*

I began badly – as though interviewing came not as naturally to a journalist as honey-gathering to a bee. And it was not so much that this was the Dublin labourer, the much-lauded tenement-dweller who has proved a second Synge, and is at the moment the prey of London lion-hunters. That might happen to anyone.

But this was the man whose *Juno and the Paycock* had proved fine enough to lead Mr George Bernard Shaw, most wise, most impatient of critics, to the box-office twice. Knowing which I could only question lamely: 'Er, er, how did you start?' and Sean O'Casey in his pleasant, almost inaudible way – a sort of brogued mutter – replied:

'Oi started as a baby; a very weak baby; a very irritable baby; and a very hungry baby. And Oi remained a very hungry choild. And still as a very hungry choild, Oi got my first job as an errand boy to an ironmonger at 4s. a week. You see, my father died when Oi was three or four years old, and so my elder brothers, who had all been fed and educated, came off better than Oi did.

'And now Oi suppose you'll be wanting to hear what Oi was doing after that. Working, sleeping, aating, drinking, cursing, starving, fighting, courting, going on strike, reading, educating myself in my leisure moments, and learning the Oirish language.

'Sometimes Oi wish Oi was a labourer again – it's a grand loife for a man – a grand loife. It gives me almost a homesickness to pass men now knocking down houses and building roads. For you can't sever yourself from humanity, for there's nothing else that counts. Didn't Synge say, "Although his head may be in the stars his roots must be in the earth"?

---

* In the following extract, the author's attempt to render O'Casey's accent is now more likely to appear offensive than evocative, but it does at least give an indication of contemporary attitudes. It also illustrates that O'Casey was well able to keep his interviewers on their toes.

'And that's my oidea of Art. There must be blood in all things that are written, in all pictures that are painted, in all songs that are sung. There must be the cry of humanity; it may be a ferocious cry, a bitter cry, an angry cry; but if it isn't a human cry it isn't Art. For loife is the primary fact.

'Yes, Oi like London and Oi like the English people Oi have met very, very much indade. But Oi couldn't live here, and Oi'm going back to Dublin soon to work. Oi'm publishing my play over here, *The Plough and the Stars*, and Oi'm dedicating it to my mother. My mother had a wonderful laugh, and Oi heard her laugh a quarter of an hour before she died. And Oi am dedicating my play "To the laugh of my mother at the Gate of the Grave . . ."'

'Sean O'Casey's Abode: His Objections to Ireland', *Irish Independent*, 7 July 1926

Sean O'Casey the Irish playwright, has parted from Dublin more in sorrow than in anger, and has taken a flat in Kensington on a three years' lease.

'I like London,' he said to a special correspondent last night, 'and London likes me. That's more than I can say of Ireland. I have a good deal of courage, but not much patience, and it takes both courage and patience to live in Ireland. The Irish have no time for those that don't agree with their ideas, and I have no time for those that don't agree with mine. So we decided to compromise and I am coming here. The English are more tolerant and they believe a lot.

'It may,' he said, 'mean three years penal servitude for me, but, begorra, it cannot be worse than Dublin.'

'The Real Sean O'Casey', by Rupert Croft-Cooke, *Theatre World*, October 1926

Now the truth about Sean O'Casey is the truth about all great men – simplicity. His absolute lack of affectation, his almost boyish unreservedness, his gutsy tolerance, may have been disappointing to reporters, but they are a confirmation of all that his plays promise. He is not a young-looking man, but he has a certain youthfulness of manner. And he gives one the impression of having passed through periods of great enthusiasms and sacrifices to a cause, and reached a state of mind when he can see the good in every cause, and can attach himself to none. He speaks of the time when he felt 'the old nationalist animus', and would only spell his name 'O'Cathasaigh' in the true Irish way, as though such hotheaded days were done. He can find something to say in defence of almost everything.

'No – I'm not a Catholic,' he smiled, 'but when you've lived and suffered and worked and starved with a people, you get to understand their religion. And there is more beauty in some of their ways than in superstitions. When a friend of mine lost a pound note in his kitchen he lit a candle to Saint Anthony – and is not that better than the folk who drive about with a dam' Teddy Bear on their cars? I was taught my Bible – I'm not sorry for that – for it's fine in places.'

That remark, it seemed to me, was a key to the beauty of much of his prose. There is almost a biblical way about some of it, and such phrases as 'Well-nigh spent' recall it, but he does not talk much of his art.

'I don't like writing,' he says. 'It may be laziness, but writing is a great labour to me. I've had enough work.'

Something in his appearance suggested that he did not exaggerate. He has the frame of a man who has really toiled, and there is nothing to make one imagine the 'author who goes among the working classes for experience'. Nothing, in other words, artificial. Something gnarled about his neck and wrists gave the impression of a man who could fell a tree. And even in his tolerance, paradoxical as it may seem, there is a hint of the aggressive. He seemed determined not to be impatient, even of faults.

Speaking of someone whom we both know, he said:

'Vain, of course, but then youth is vain. I smiled at the way he carried his stick and his gloves and things, but then I've known some filthy swine in the Labour Party and some fine fellows over-dressed.'

Of Art he has thought and felt a great deal.

'Goya is my great man,' he said, 'and most of the old Italians leave me cold. I admire Botticelli and Augustus John's pictures enormously, too.' That he liked Goya was, I suppose, only to be expected, and his remarking on it brought one to the sudden realisation that his plays really are Goya pictures. The famous looting scene in *The Plough and the Stars* is all Goya.

'Have I ever known what it is to be hungry? Have I ever known anything else for the last fifteen years?' (I wish I could reproduce his brogue.) 'It's true what I tell you. You get used to hunger, and a good many other things. If you live in a tenement you get used to almost anything – the chap from upstairs coming in drunk and calling you every name under the sun and offering to cut your throat, then round next morning to apologise; or the furniture and everything in the room upstairs being flung out of the window; or boiling your food in an empty sardine tin. But you can be further down and out than a tenement. I've slept in doss-houses where the beds are six deep one above the other, and a ladder for reaching them.'

Of Irish authors he has definite opinions – believes in James Joyce, but not, I felt, in T. C. Murray,* and liked the elegance of Wilde. He has read enormously, but, I should gather, erratically. And above all, I should think he is one of the most independent men alive. Sean O'Casey 'does not give a damn'.

* T. C. Murray (1873–1959) was one of the so-called 'Cork realists', whose plays, including *Birthright* (1911) and *Aftermath* (1922), dealt with the social and religious restrictions affecting rural communities.

'Sean O'Casey or a Rough Diamond', from *Are They the Same At Home? Being a Series of Bouquets Diffidently Distributed* (1927), by Beverley Nichols*

He had on a new sky-blue overcoat, and as he took it off, flinging it over the back of his chair, I observed a lining fiercely decorated with red squares. Upon this coat he proceeded to lay his cap, which was of a lighter shade of blue. He then sat down, and buried his face in his hands.

I had lured him to a tea-shop. He had a distinct distaste for more exalted places. The tea-shop was filled with a smell of steam and stale rock-cakes. The waitress raced about, carrying the rock-cakes to pale young men and girls who were seated around us. I have never known a more noisy place. The roar of traffic (which ever and anon increased to deafening point as the door swung open to admit more pale young men), the clattering of tea-cups, the low, moaning conversation of the customers.

Yet it was in such a place that a spell was woven over me by Sean O'Casey, with the weak eyes, the deep-lined cheeks, and the human mouth. It made me forget the noise, the flash of buses outside the dirty windows, everything, except that I was in the presence of a great man. They brought us muffins, and tea, and a plate of cakes; such cakes – cakes like dead sea anemones, with frills round them, cakes with decorations of marzipan and stale cream clinging to them like alien growths. O'Casey looked up and took some tea and a muffin.

'Yesterday,' he said, 'was the happiest day I've spent since I came to England. It was in Hyde Park that I spent it, and I stood there listening to the speakers. I felt almost drunk at the end of it – the characters up there are so rich in comedy.

* Beverley Nichols (1898–1983) was a prolific journalist and well-known society figure of the inter-war years. Having published his first novel while still an undergraduate, and evidently something of a dandy (he was allegedly the first man at Oxford to wear suede shoes), he was, as this interview illustrates, in many respects the antithesis of the down-to-earth O'Casey.

'*What are your dramatists doing to neglect Hyde Park?*' He smacked his fist on the table, and pointed his muffin at me like a limp bludgeon. I regarded it, fascinated, but did not reply. Then he leant back, his head turned slightly to one side, looked at me out of the corner of his eye, and smiled. 'Why, young man, it's the finest field of character you'll ever know. The people I saw there last night. You listen.'

He bent forward again, and spoke almost in a whisper. 'There was a woman there, a fine woman, standing in the lamplight under the trees. Her voice was very clear and sweet, and she didn't care how many times they interrupted her. All the time she spoke she was patting the crucifix by her side – patting it, fondling it . . . like this . . .

'There was a man there who made a speech about milk. As I stood in the crowd I knew, as soon as he had begun, that he had been making the same speech for years, winter and summer, morning and night. For the people in the front row of the crowd knew it by heart and began to repeat it with him . . . He didn't care. He went on – with his chorus. There's a tragedy, and there's a comedy . . .

'There was a man with a bald head, and little glistening eyes, who spoke of Jesus. There was the light of madness in his eyes, and as I watched him I saw right deep into him, and I knew that he would have killed anybody who refused to be led to Jesus – killed him and thanked God for the opportunity . . .

'Then there was a thin man in a black coat, and long grey hair, who kept on taking oranges out of his pocket. He was a vegetarian. There was a man with a mournful voice who spoke of the Lost Tribes. There was every sort of religious mania, dietic [*sic*] mania, political mania, personal mania. And there it all goes on, night after night, under the trees. But nobody seems to notice it. None of those characters is ever put on the stage. Why? Tell me why?'

My muffin had now set quite solid, and, on being prodded, felt less obscene than when it first arrived. But I was not really interested in muffins. For opposite me was O'Casey, the ex-

29

slum boy, in 'smart' London. Here he was, with his genius of observation, seeing for the first time the painted ladies, the crimped young men, the poisoned critics, the wilting hectic generation which we have now come to know so well. I was intensely anxious to know how it all struck him. And, in order to find out, I asked him about the work of a very brilliant young English dramatist who has specialized in the portrayal of this particular stratum of society.

'Did you ever see [Noel Coward's] *The Vortex*?' I asked O'Casey.

'No. But I read it.'

'Didn't you think it a fine play?'

'No.' Rather fiercely he put five lumps of sugar into his tea-cup. 'The people in it are absolutely artificial.'

'But they're meant to be artificial. If he'd drawn them in any other way, he'd have been telling lies.'

'Nobody's artificial.' O'Casey looked at me kindly, rather as though I were a child who could not quite understand why $a \times a = a^2$.

'Nobody's artificial,' he said. 'Even insects aren't artificial. Shakespeare drew artificial characters, but he gave them humanity. My point about these people is that they haven't got humanity.'

I began to grow almost excited. 'I know they haven't got humanity. They haven't got it on the stage (at least in the first two acts), and they haven't got it in real life. You haven't met them, that's all. I shouldn't think you particularly wanted to. But if you did meet them, you'd realize what I said was true.'

'If I *did* meet them,' he answered, 'I shouldn't listen to them when they talked like that. I should take them home. I may sit next to a woman at lunch who talks to me politely, and says all the right things. Perhaps she says them very cleverly, but her remarks don't interest me. *She* doesn't begin to live till you see her alone, within four walls. Then she drops all her poses, and she tells you her son is going to marry a woman she hates, or that her lover has left her. She shows all her greed, her vanities (her *true* vanities), she shows you the things you can love about her, and the things you can hate about her. Isn't that more interesting than mere pose?'

I was not daunted even yet.

'I believe,' I said, 'that there are people would pose just as much alone as at a luncheon party. Their whole life is pose. You may say that you would see through their poses. How could you, if the pose was *them*? As one poses, one becomes.'

'I don't believe any human being is devoid of humanity,' said O'Casey. 'If you do, then you're wrong. There's no such thing as inherent artificiality. That's the trouble about half the dramatists today. *They're making life out of drama, instead of making drama out of life.*'

I dropped the point. If there had not been so many crashes going on behind, and if I had not been feeling particularly disillusioned that afternoon, as though I were dwelling in a world of masks, I might have got nearer to an agreement with him. But I still feel he has not yet met these characters which he says are 'artificial,' which, to you and me, are so distressingly real.

'The Silver Tassie: Interview with Mr Sean O'Casey', by G. W. B., Observer, 6 October 1929

The Story of Mr Sean O'Casey is a modern epic: the Dublin labourer who, after spending night after night at the Abbey Theatre, eventually wrote plays which are among the greatest of the century. I had seen him on the stage when, after one of his first nights, the immaculately dressed, urbane manager introduced a shy young man in a tweed suit and cardigan, who blinked at the audience and then fled into the wings. Last week I saw him again in his own home at St John's Wood, where for two hours he talked to me about his own and other people's plays – mostly the latter.

The first impression on entering the room was of the magnificent Augustus John portrait over the mantelpiece, and the second was that everything else approximated in taste to the picture. The books on the shelves were Shakespeare and the other Elizabethan playwrights, volumes of the Restoration dramatists, Balzac, Nietzsche. Then O'Casey came in. He was dressed in a grey sweater, and I realised how remarkably John had caught the man in the portrait.

We began, of course, with *The Silver Tassie*, which Mr C. B. Cochran is presenting at the Apollo on Friday night. He was full of enthusiasm for Mr Cochran, 'That rare combination of artist and man of the theatre,' for Mr Raymond Massey, who is producing *The Tassie* (as he calls it) and 'enters more fully into the play than I do myself', and for Mr Charles Laughton, and the rest of the company. 'It is a difficult play,' he said, 'because in one of the scenes I have attempted something which has never been done on the stage before. One of Mr Yeats's objections to the play was that it contained no dominating character, and for that reason I feel it is a better play than *Juno and the Paycock* (which is the poorest thing I have had produced) and *The Plough and the Stars*. In *The Tassie* the tragedy dominates the characters.

'Although the full correspondence with the Abbey Theatre has been published certain newspapers have recently stated that *The Silver Tassie* was not produced in Dublin because I refused to accept Mr Yeats's suggestions and make some alterations in the play. In other words, they make me out an impossible creature. I should be glad if you will correct this. In his letter to me written on 20 April, 1928, Mr Yeats said: "I cannot advise you to amend the play . . . I see nothing for it but a new theme." I am anxious to make it clear that I am not a high-and-mighty dramatist who thinks that his plays cannot be improved. On the first night it will be seen that certain of Mr Massey's suggestions have been accepted; the production will differ slightly from the version published by Macmillan.

'I was interested in St. John Ervine's article in last Sunday's *Observer* on the use of the aside in modern drama. Playwrights and managers are afraid of so many things and think too much of their audiences. They are afraid of soliloquy and pause in drama, and I believe that audiences are not as stupid as dramatists imagine. I am irritated by being told of the things I must not do in plays.'

I asked him if he had written any new plays.

'I am incapable of starting a new play until the last one is produced. After *The Silver Tassie* is staged I shall lose interest in it, except that it provides me with money (and I want money as much as anybody), and start on something else. I have two or three ideas, and one came when I watched the supers* during the rehearsals for *The Tassie*. I am writing some short stories based on characters I have met. Some time ago I started to turn *Juno* into a novel, but I dropped it, I couldn't do it. I have also written part of an autobiography, which will be finished and published some time.'

We talked of modern dramatists. 'England is waiting for the great English dramatist who will write about his own people. The playwrights of today turn out tiny plays about little society ladies and gentlemen with scraps of photographic dialogue. They throw life out of focus. Hardly any of them attempt to portray the life of today with imagination and passion. Recently I read in an article which offered advice to young playwrights that Mr Noel Coward and Mr Frederick Lonsdale† should be studied. Shakespeare, the Elizabethans, the Restoration dramatists, and Shaw are the men to study.

'I would make it a penal offence,' Mr O'Casey continued, 'for any man to write a play without being able to declaim two or three of Shakespeare's plays by heart. Shakespeare was my education. When I was a boy in Dublin thirty years ago, the Benson Company‡ came to the city, and I spent all my small

---

* 'Supers' is a contraction of 'supernumeraries', meaning 'extras'.
† Frederick Lonsdale (1881–1954) had begun his writing career producing librettos for musical comedies, later moving on to write social comedies, including *The Last of Mrs Cheyney* (1925) and *Aren't We All?*, which was revived in 1929, the year of this interview.
‡ Sir Frank Benson's touring company presented George Moore and W. B. Yeats's *Diarmuid and Grania* at the Gaiety Theatre in Dublin in 1901, and it seems possible that this experimental play was seen by O'Casey.

wages and went without food in order to see all the plays that were performed. I could hardly read or write at the time.'

'That was your first interest in the drama?' I asked.

'Yes, I suppose it was in me, somehow. I learned to read by Shakespeare and used to act the plays in my room' – here O'Casey gave me a scene from *Julius Caesar* – 'and when I was seventeen, I wrote a comedy called *Withered Heather*. Some time after that I belonged to the drama group in the National Club. The members were content to imitate the Abbey Players, perform the same plays, in order to become little Arthur Sinclairs.* I suggested that it would be a good idea to play something that had never been acted before, and I wrote *Frost and the Flower* . . . That was really my start.'

'Remembrance of Things Past II: On Meeting Sean O'Casey', by Leslie Rees, *Meanjin Quarterly*, Melbourne, December 1964

In London [in 1930], after months of delay, some impulse caused me not to write but to take a bus to St John's Wood and knock at his front door. It was a solid ugly door on an unattractive semi-detached house built close to the street. A middle-aged woman opened the door. From her voice and manner I judged her an Irish servant but I couldn't be sure. I asked to see Mr O'Casey. After some delay – during which I was able to note that the walls of the passage-hall were hung with large reproductions of paintings by Degas, Gaugin and Van Gogh – an attractive young woman came and said that she was Mrs O'Casey. I introduced myself and said that, having had a letter from O'Casey, I hoped to be able to meet him. Keeping me on the front mat she went away, then returned and said in a rather business-like way, the way of an important person's wife: 'Mr

* Francis Quinton McDonnell (1883–1951), whose stage name was Arthur Sinclair, was a member of the Abbey Company between 1904 and 1912, and was known for what was evidently a bravura and idiosyncratic performance style.

O'Casey is writing now: would you like to come here for tea on Sunday? I'll try to get him away from his work for an hour.' Dancing with unbelief I groped my way toward the bus stop.

On Sunday at 4 p.m. I was on the doorstep again and the servant-dear immediately led me into a small lounge room, furnished with comfortable, modern-minded settee and armchairs . . . In a quiet unassertive mumbling tone O'Casey motioned me to a seat. He seemed to be trying to get the hang of me. 'So you've come all the way from Australia?' The voice was raw Dublin, thin and whining, not attractive like the best Irish tones. 'Tell me about Australia.' He relaxed on a sofa and put his feet up. I could hardly believe my ears. Here in England a resident was asking me to talk about Australia. This had scarcely happened before: the even unruffled capacity of the English educated classes for *not* being curious about a stranger and his background was one of the things that most defeated me. It appeared at once that O'Casey, although living on English soil, was far from being absorbed into English ways. I looked with growing appreciation at his rough and ugly face, his thin denuded cheeks, his long protruding nose and the untidy hair that was mousy in front and skimpy-bald on the back of the skull.

About Australia he seemed to know nothing except the geographical position. This ignorance was no novelty in Britain so a few facts lubricated the opening movements of our conversation. Before long his wife came in, chic and dainty, with her West End voice that was not quite West End. And the wordless old duck of a servant brought in the afternoon tea.

Mrs O'Casey was addressed by her husband as Eileen. She scarcely seemed true to the expected picture. O'Casey must have been about forty-six years of age, she about twenty-six. Was she part of the fruits of his success? Such a person did not seem to have emerged from a tenement background. From conversation she would be Irish-born but the manner was English. They spoke of a boy, aged about eighteen months. In fact the boy was now to be seen in the back garden, looked after by a nurse. The patterns were neither slum Dublin nor standard St John's Wood. But despite discrepancies all was domestic harmony and light. O'Casey showed a lively interest in his son. So did I, always a good move in people's homes I'd found. Eileen revealed that she was an actress and singer. At present she had a chorus part in the long-running Noel Coward musical *Bitter-Sweet*.

My 'hour' was slipping away in small talk not connected with O'Casey's plays. I wanted to steer him on to this vital subject but he was reluctant, bored with it. He talked warmly and abundantly and with a broad simpleness about other people's plays and books, using his low mumbly voice not very eloquently but always with decision. Shakespeare came into the talk often: O'Casey was all for quoting long passages from *Hamlet* and *Julius Caesar* but usually dried up after a few pentameters and turned to me with the words, 'What is it? What is it?' an appeal that to my chagrin I never seemed to be able to gratify. Sometimes in quoting he would interpolate, 'There's a lovely loine,' the brogue now coming over more richly as he smiled and peered in my direction.

When at last I asked, 'Do you think *Juno* the best of your plays?' he said in an offhand way: 'No. I hate *Juno*. Tired of it. *The Silver Tassie* every time.' He went on denigrating *Juno and the Paycock*. He was tired of making characters like Captain Boyle and Mrs Madigan . . . too easy. It was the purpose in his work he found hard to express.

I reflected that in one act of *The Silver Tassie* O'Casey had become the consciously literary playwright, no longer using the Dublin vernacular heightened by his native gift for humour and rhythm: rather going after inner revelation by poetic statement. Any author would have been stimulated by such adventures in stylistic writing: O'Casey was much involved with them now, not that he seemed able or had the desire to discuss them in detail.

I mentioned the question of facility. His plays, I said, seemed to flow along in tidal waves of energy. 'Wrong,' he said. Writing was a great labour. It took him twelve months of spare time to write *Juno*. He further illustrated his pondering thought and trial-by-error craftsmanship by telling how, when some alterations were required during rehearsals of *The Tassie*, he had to bring the script home before he could adjust it. 'Somerset Maugham would have slipped the new words in on the spot,' he said.

We discussed plays recently on in London. He denounced *Journey's End*. 'A bad play!' I had been brought under its spell and felt bound to defend it. 'It's a bad play,' O'Casey repeated, his voice rising in anger. The taste of lemon came into my mouth. 'It's a good play,' I said with equal vehemence. 'It's a *bad* play,' said O'Casey crushingly.

He did not give reasons. Afterwards I reflected that his dislike of *Journey's End* could have come from the class-conscious element in Sherriff's outlook, implying, or running the risk of implying, that the only soldiers worth taking seriously were the officers, not the rank and file. O'Casey's own bitter war scene in *The Tassie* was of course markedly different, although criticised by Yeats as not based on personal experience and therefore not good. Any comparative thoughts on the subject of *The Tassie* were unstated but the sparks had flown between us for a few seconds and I wondered whether O'Casey was now going to throw me out as a cheeky young intruder. But conversation resumed and no harm done.

There was another slight passage of hackling warmth when the baby was once more mentioned. Mrs O'Casey on slight encouragement told me of the child's bright ways and O'Casey during this period sat in silence. Suddenly he said with trenchant vigour: 'And we won't be sending him to one of those damned universities.' I demurred, being fresh from a university myself, though I'd been but a humble part-time student earning my way. 'No university education,' said O'Casey dangerously. 'Hotbeds of snobbery for the privileged classes.' I asked leave to tell something about the University of Western Australia where at that time no fees were charged any scholar and anybody from the entire state population was welcome provided he could pass his examinations. O'Casey was impressed: he cooled down and finished by mumbling: 'Well, it might be a good thing for him to go to that sort of university after all . . . it might be good for him to mix with different people like that.' I felt I'd won a worthwhile round.

At about six o'clock Mrs O'Casey seemed to grow restive so I said, 'I'd better be going now.' But O'Casey at once put in, 'Come up to my room for half an hour.' I said, 'So long as I'm not in the way,' and O'Casey replied, with humorous direct-ness, 'We'll tell you when you're in the way.' His wife there-upon asked me if I'd like to stay to dinner. I was certainly anxious to probe into more of the O'Casey story though with-out thought of journalistic exploitation. The O'Caseys were not treating me as an interviewer.

O'Casey and I now went upstairs to a little room, furnished with shelves of books (there were two full bookcases down-stairs), a small desk, an armchair and a narrow bed against one wall. He said, from between lips that hardly moved, 'This is where I work.' I sat in the armchair and had a cigarette and O'Casey lolled at full length on the bed: at that moment he hardly looked the hard-toiling type.

I eventually persuaded him to talk about the subject of his plays and he told me the story of his beginnings. There was the first book he wrote, a little history of the trades union move-ment.* 'I got £15 for that and the cheque came as my mother lay dead. I couldn't get it changed, people thought it suspicious I should have had a cheque for so much money, in fact a cheque at all. It was crossed and had to be paid into a bank and I hadn't a bank account. A friend got it changed and most of it went on the funeral. When the undertaker came to the house he said, "No bloody money, no bloody funeral." Just like that. But I had the money.' . . .

---

* From O'Casey's response, it would appear that the interviewer is actually referring to The Story of the Irish Citizen Army. See Introduction.

Despite rancorous moments he'd been a much milder man than I had expected, with touches of gentleness and courtesy, a rough diamond only by bourgeois English standards. There had been few outbursts of spirits of energy to reflect the boisterous humour of his plays. During the whole evening, I don't think he once laughed aloud, though ironic comedy expressed itself in wry verbal comment. He seemed far from physically strong, was even frail, flat-chested. But his positive nature revealed itself through his sense of enquiry, his spontaneous curiosity. As to the reticent anglo-saxon middle-class life that was all around us, obviously he was a fish out of its true element. For want of a better, he had immersed himself in another element which he was prepared to accept but not necessarily to approve. At mention of cricket test matches he at once made it clear that he backed the Australians: this merely out of an Irishman's automatic rejection of England. I am sure that our common lack of liking for the alien English caste system was a bond between him and me. Egalitarian Australianism matched egalitarian Irishism. On the way home I couldn't have felt more exhilarated.

'Some Dramatists', from No Phantoms Here (1932), by J. L. Hodson*

Six years ago I was sent to Dublin . . . Having a few hours to spare, I sought Sean O'Casey. He had never been to England then nor had his *Juno and the Paycock* been performed in London. I paid two visits to the Abbey Theatre before I got his address – O'Casey didn't like to be called on in his tenement lodging, they said – he would probably be annoyed. I walked up and down the North Circular Road which seemed about five miles long this grey afternoon with mist curling in the shadows. Shopkeepers and drovers had never heard of him. They knew of

* Although primarily a journalist, Hodson also wrote plays, including *The Back Way* (1927) and *These Fathers* (1930).

O'Caseys who drove tramcars, or slaughtered cattle, or sold newspapers, or laboured at the docks, but O'Caseys who wrote plays, 'Sure, they'd never heard of such a t'ing. Wouldn't it be Shamus O'Casey who played the cornet I'd be wantin'?'

About five o'clock I found the house – a tall, gloomy house, dirty grey, with peeling plaster, and stone passage – the sort you find in any slum. I knocked at the first door down the hall on the left. A man in shirt-sleeves opened it about six inches. Was he Sean O'Casey? He was. Could I speak to him? He didn't think so – he was getting dressed. I told him who I was. He was not impressed by me or by my newspaper, the *Daily Mail*. He had no time to talk about plays – he was going down town to see a girl. But I hadn't tramped up and down the five-miles-long North Circular Road for nothing. I kept on talking and O'Casey's natural courtesy gave in.

It was a curious meeting. He continued in the half dark groping about, getting dressed, and I sat down and fired questions at him . . . He tore the world's hypocrisies – besides handfuls of contemporaries – to pieces with searing, cynical tongue and bitter humour. He thought little in those days of folk like Noel Coward and John Galsworthy. 'You can't turn life into a comedy in one play and into a tragedy in another,' he said. 'Life isn't like that. We have our happy moments and our sad moments'; and again he said, 'If you want to find the play that is in people, you must follow them home.' He used the words of a writer and the accent of a workman, a soft, broad, Irish brogue.

In this room he slept, ate, worked and lived his life, cooking his meals himself – a piece of bacon, a few potatoes. He had an old tall typewriter, bought second-hand, and home-made bookshelves crammed with books – Shakespeare, the first book he ever bought, Milton – stuff like that. His desk he carried home in three pieces to save cartage.

I said, 'They say you break all the rules in writing a play.'

'So did Shakespeare,' he said, thrusting out his sharp chin and peering at me from short-sighted, weak eyes . . . His first success was *The Shadow of a Gunman*, written largely out of his own experience. But it wasn't until *Juno* caught on that he gave up his manual work. 'I decided then', he said, 'that one job is enough for any man.'

I asked him if he had any idea how much he was likely to earn if *Juno* proved a success in London. No, he had no idea . . . O'Casey was doing a small amount of prose-writing for the Irish weeklies, but when I mentioned novel-writing he was scornful. No, he would never write a novel; any damn fool could write a novel. (A few months later I told Arnold Bennett, sitting in the stalls of a theatre, what O'Casey said. He looked solemnly to his front and said, with his stammer, '*I* don't find is so-so-so-damned easy.') By this time we had tramped to the middle of Dublin and O'Casey left me abruptly to keep his appointment in a tea-shop, this bachelor of forty-one whose genius was flowering.

Next time I saw him was a few months ago. He met me as I got off a bus at the corner of a lane in Chalfont St. Giles, Buckinghamshire. I had written asking him if I might visit him, for I was eager to know what he was doing, and I found him awaiting me. As I rode down I had pondered about him. Since we had met he had been awarded the Hawthornden Prize for *Juno*, had failed to write *The Red Lily*, a play about a prostitute that he had told me in Dublin was to be his next work, and had had his *Silver Tassie* rejected by the Abbey Theatre and produced by C. B. Cochran. And after that – silence. No play from O'Casey. Had his genius deserted him, his inspiration dried up now Dublin was left behind. Or was it going into his tongue instead of his pen?

I saw a man standing there and for a moment hesitated. He wore a wideawake hat, a brown guernsey to the throat like a fisherman, a Harris tweed suit, and strong boots. He looked at me from behind gold-rimmed spectacles, we spoke and turned down the road. 'Watch the way,' he said. 'I can't see well enough to come back with you after dark.'

A swan sailed the wayside pond, smoke curled in the windless air above the brown brick cottages, and there was the smell of burning wood and rubbish. He told me with deep content that England is lovely beyond his belief, that he likes the quiet, sober people. No, he would never go back to Dublin except on a visit. We passed John Milton's cottage; William Penn's house, he said, was over the hill.* On a small rising stood his brick bungalow, with two acres of ground and an orchard. O'Casey likes to dig there and work in the garden, and when he isn't digging or walking about the countryside to work at his old desk on the old typewriter . . . I thought his tongue was keen but less saw-edged, his humour as deep but with greater breadth than when we had met in Dublin. He looked well and talked, with something of the air of a master, of plays, books, films and wireless. Would wireless develop into an art form? He doubted it. Had I heard the broadcast performance of *Julius Caesar* the other night? He thought it was terrible. He had sung a Litany calling down the wrath o'God on them.

I asked him where *The Red Lily* was, and what he was working at. He laughed that I had been taken in. There never had been a *Red Lily*, he said, nor was there ever such a play in his intention. He had told people that to put them off – they were always pestering him in those days. One may add they still do. Every time anything is said about his working on a play people write asking if they may see it. I found he has kept an Irish and boyish love of being contrary and says a good many things for devilment; and that he is disputatious and fond of argument.

He didn't want to talk about his work, but he owned he is writing a new play about London life; which part of London he wouldn't say. First, he said, he thought he would write it straight for the films, but again he changed his mind. He is half-way through a sort of biography too, and has done a number of sketches – 'weaving a pattern' he called it. He works very slowly, writing and re-writing – never pens even a letter without great care.

* John Milton (1608–74), English poet and essayist, retired to Chalfont in 1665. William Penn (1644–1718) lived at Rickmansworth, six miles from Chalfont St Giles, following his marriage in 1672. He later gave his name to the American state of Pennsylvania.

Six years ago he had told me he could write plays better because he was never educated; now he described that as nonsense. 'Even now,' he said, 'I don't know the English language.' I asked him which part of the day he does his writing in, but it was his wife who answered. 'He starts about mid-night,' she said, 'and goes on tap-tapping at the machine till two or three in the morning.'

We had tea, and his son Brian [*sic*], aged three, extremely Irish-looking, came in and looked around with the wise comprehension of that age and departed without speaking.

Mrs O'Casey said, 'Sean has read your play. Ask him what he thinks about it.' But he demurred. 'I don't like reading work by men I'm going to meet, especially plays. I wouldn't like to express any opinion that might influence them.' We talked a good deal after tea. He seems to have no doubts about anything and I suspect that when he has, he becomes even more downright to entertain you or stir you up.

Here are some of his assertions:

That we need a chain of municipal theatres.

That he is sick of people talking about *Juno and the Paycock* – 'It was a good enough play for a man just beginning, but no more than that';

That our finest English dramatist today is Granville-Barker;*

That he can find Joxer Dalys (one of his *Juno* characters) – wheedling, drunken, deceitful, cowardly – anywhere;

That he's finished with Dublin as a play subject – 'To be creative, you must pass on to something fresh';

That he can't be bothered to insert emendations to *The Silver Tassie* – which he admits has its faults;

That you can't write except from within your experience, and that Shakespeare and Milton were no exception to that;

That a newspaper has more abiding influence on people than a war;

* Harley Granville-Barker (1877–1946) was a prominent playwright, director and actor, whose plays, including *The Voysey Inheritance* (1905), *Waste* (1907) and *The Madras House* (1910), dealt with social and sexual inequality.

That no young dramatist should take advice from an older one;

That the old novel form is dead and that the few writers really 'alive' include James Joyce and Aldous Huxley;

That the theatre also needs a new art form;

That a hard upbringing is no help to a writer, but the contrary . . .

He was almost gay when, taking his wife's arm to guide him, the two of them walked back to the bus with me. I said, 'I could have sworn that in Dublin your eyes were brown. And now they are blue. Was I mistaken?'

No, it was very likely so, he said. They change colour with the treatment for his short-sightedness. Blue is their true colour. 'You know,' his wife said, 'Sean was practically blind for years and had his eyes bandaged. He puts that down to being half-starved as a boy.' His greatest joys happen to be reading Shakespeare and looking at good pictures, so it's a particularly harsh stroke that Fate has dealt him. Yet he not only made no mention of that but struck me as being profoundly content; and he made me proud of our English countryside and its people who have influenced him so. He sees men working on the road – one of his old jobs – and a rush of the old wish to be with them comes over him. 'Every man should work with his hands three months in every twelve,' he said, as we trudged through the darkness.

We stood waiting for the bus. The night wind was chill and he had no overcoat. I asked them not to wait – he would catch cold. But he had strong views on that, too – 'No man,' he said, 'can catch cold by going without his shirt. I've tried it and proved it' – and he would not be shaken on the point.

The bus swung round the corner, lights blazing. 'Oh,' I said, 'I've forgotten to ask you what your ambitions are.'

'Ambitions?' he grinned. 'That the next may be a great play – and *not* to send the boy to Oxford.'

'Who is Then the Gentleman? A Few Notes on Sean
O'Casey', by Bosley Crowther, *New York Times*, 14
October 1934

It had been carefully explained beforehand that Sean O'Casey,
the Irish dramatist and author of the play *Within the Gates*,
which will have its New York première next week at the
National Theatre, preferred not to be disturbed – especially by
strangers – during rehearsals. It was a justifiable preference. He
desired to be alone and unmolested, free to concentrate his
sense upon the stage. Only by special dispensation was an
inquisitive visitor granted permission one day last week to
intrude upon his solitude.

But when the visitor arrived at the theatre Mr O'Casey was
nowhere to be found. He had apparently impelled himself by
some Celtic charm to vanish. No one seemed to know where
he had gone. On the stage a young woman director was mar-
shalling a sombre procession of ten or twelve actors and
actresses across an inclined platform behind the figure of a
massive war memorial. They were the Down-and-Outers
within the gates and they chanted a sonorous dirge as they
plodded disconsolately along. Mr O'Casey was not among
them. Nor had he yet appeared when the young director
called a sudden halt of the procession, bitingly reproved her
charges for not convincing her of their desolation, apparently, and then dismissed them for luncheon. The morning
rehearsal was ended.

Then, from the wings of the stage and as casual as one might
please, there strolled a lean, raw-boned man of more than
medium height. It was, of course, Mr O'Casey . . . His complete informality was perfect – so perfect, in fact, that one liked
him before a word was spoken. It was easy to perceive why this
man, when he first went to London from Ireland's Abbey
Theatre as a new dramatic 'lion', had refused to array himself
in dress clothes or formal dinner parties. He was too obviously
comfortable in the ones he was wearing. And when he did

speak the richness of his Irish brogue and the low modulation of his voice were as warm as a Dublin snug.

The visitor admitted quite frankly that he had come on a somewhat impudent mission – to find out, in brief, what sort of man this playwright, O'Casey, is. A slow smile spread over his face.

'I've been married for seven years,' said he, 'and my wife doesn't yet know what sort of man I am.'

A friend, standing by, suggested that it takes eight tailors to make a man.

'Nine, isn't it?' corrected Mr O'Casey. 'But the Lord knows how many it takes to make an author!'

With the opportunity abandoned of seeing the author in immediate contact with his play – a play, incidentally, which has been hailed by drama critics who have read the script as a profound masterpiece – it was proposed that the visitor sit down with Mr O'Casey in an adjoining room for a chat. That was all right with the latter. Any place would do. And, there being only one chair in the room, he offered to sit on the floor. The contingency, however, was avoided.

The 'chat' – which eventually became a two-hour debate on most of the currently popular subjects and wove its way out of the theatre into a convenient tavern and back to the theatre again – was temporarily held up while an agent for the producers endeavoured to arrange a convenient time in which another visitor might see O'Casey. A 'gentleman', the agent described him.

Mr O'Casey shot a sidelong glance from under the visor of his cap.

'When Adam delved and Eve span, who was then the gentleman?' he parried. 'Who *is* then the gentleman? I thought the only gentlemen were in England.'

The appointment was finally arranged, after considerable banter on the author's part – banter, the tenor of which was mostly an objection that no pretty women were ever brought around to interview him. Then the agent departed and the present visitor observed that Mr O'Casey seemed to enjoy his little joke.

'Did you think I was joking?' he innocently inquired. 'That's the funny thing – when an Irishman is serious people think he is joking, and when he jokes they think he's serious.'

His face assumed an expression of perturbation as the visitor asked whether Irishmen are ever serious.

'Serious! Man, I should say so! There's no more sincere people in the world than the Irish. Why an Irishman would murder his own father or brother over a difference in creed or politics! If you want more evidence of sincerity than that, I don't know where you can find it.'

The conversation thereupon turned to a serious discussion of the theatre – after digressing hither and yon over one or two incidental subjects. The objection which Mr O'Casey has to the so-called realistic theatre was not long in manifesting itself, and the visitor, mindful of the celebrated debate which raged between the playwright and the Irish poet George Russell ('AE')* over a matter of artistic standards, was discreetly receptive.

He had seen several of Broadway's current attractions since his arrival in New York, some three weeks ago – named those he could remember with a tone of distaste – but could say very little for any of them. The fashionable drawing-room comedy which invariably treats of sex was particularly open to his barbs.

'It may be a beautiful and useful thing to turn a stage into a drawing-room,' said he, 'but to turn a drawing-room into a stage is neither beautiful nor useful. The trouble is that these bloody men writing today don't know how to put one word to another. They have no vocabulary. There's not a line of poetry from one end of their plays to the other.'

But Shakespeare, Sheridan, Ibsen in some of his plays, Shaw – he named those and several others slowly, deliberately – ah,

---

* George Russell (1867–1935), whose poetry appeared under the name 'AE', was an associate of Yeats's and an important figure in the early twentieth-century Irish revival.

but they wrote poetry for the stage! To cite his point Mr O'Casey recited the opening lines from *King Richard III* – 'Now is the winter of our discontent,' etc. He rose from his chair, dropped his cap on a table, took a turn of the room and sat down again.

'Why should an author write for the stage in the way that people talk?' he asked. 'Is there anything beautiful in ordinary conversation – the sort of things that you and I are saying now? If I had the characters in my plays speak as Irishmen ordinarily speak, I'd be writing rubbish. I get a copper phrase and do my best to turn it into gold.'

'Playwright and Box Office', *The Listener*, 7 July 1938, discussion between Maurice Browne* and Sean O'Casey

BROWNE: *I know, Sean, that anyhow you are going to bruise my English head with your Irish heel, so, just to annoy you, I'll start by suggesting that the theatre, the playwright, and the box office are, as a matter of fact, whatever they should be in theory, the only possible ruling trinity in the theatrical world today with economic conditions as they are – I don't say as they should be or as you and I would have them in our pet private Utopia.*

O'CASEY: Believe you me, I don't want to go dreaming in any Utopian land: but I do want to walk in the region of common-sense. We can't have perfection yet, but we can become a little better than we are. It is an unholy trinity, with the box office controlling the theatre and modelling the playwright. The trinity of the theatre used to be the author, the actors, and the audience; but now it is the box office, the manager, and last, of course, the playwright, so that the theatre and drama not only do not come into the sun, but do not even come into the limelight. This devotion to the box office is not only making it

* Maurice Browne (1881–1955), was an actor, producer and theatre manager in both the United States and Great Britain. He produced R. C. Sherriff's *Journey's End* in 1929 and at the time of this conversation with O'Casey was manager of the Queen's Theatre in the West End.

more difficult for the English drama as a whole, it is also making it more difficult for the box office itself. Managers are now so eager to get a success that to win one they will rook the box office of every penny it possesses. The more eager they are for a success, the more difficult a success becomes because of the cost. When a play is written, the first thought is: what is it going to cost? The question of money, money is at the head and tail of it and in the very heart of all things connected with the putting on of a bad play or a good play. When a play's doing well, the box office is a haven of light and hilarity; when a play's doing badly, the box office is a place of desolation. So we see what a mill-stone round the neck of a manager the box office really is, for so much money is lavished even on a trivial play to make it into what is called a wow, that the very success desired becomes the next thing to impossibility. And once a manager is unfortunate enough to make a pile of money out of some play, he immediately loses all he has gained by his frantic efforts to make a second pile.

Of course, you've got me when you talk about managers unfortunate enough to make a pile out of one play and idiots enough to lose it over others. I'm a bad case in point, as you know, you old rascal! But, joking apart, if you are going to buy a motorcar, or a wireless set, or a teething ring for the baby, isn't one of the very first questions you ask yourself: 'How much will it cost?' and the next question: 'Can I afford it?' I absolutely agree with you that the question of money is at the head and the tail of play production, but isn't the question of money also at the head and the tail of birth and death of every single solitary thing in between? And do you really think that this fact has such a bad influence on the playwright?

A very bad influence indeed. Everything is against the playwright who thinks of his play, and everything in favour of the playwright who thinks of the box office; and woe unto him who does, for the playwright who thinks of the box office can never write a fine play.

Half-a-minute: what about Shakespeare, for example, or Euripides, or Chekhov, or Eugene O'Neill, or even one or two Irishmen I could mention – George Bernard Shaw for example, to say nothing of the author of Juno and the Paycock? *Now, Sean, you just said, 'The playwright who thinks of the box office can never write a fine play.' Can you give any real reason for saying that?*

Of course I can. When a playwright thinks of the box office while he's writing a play, he's bound to try to model his play on the traditions with which the managers and actors are familiar. So, from the very start, he dare not write anything new. Anything new makes a play more difficult for the manager, more difficult for the actors, more difficult for the producer, and, most of all, more difficult for the poor old box office. As for Shakespeare, his best works prove that while he was writing them, he couldn't have been dreaming of the box office. The length and power of the principal characters stand in the way of a long run, and without a long run there can be no success within the calculation of the box office. The parts of Hamlet, Othello, and Lear, are so huge and call for such tremendous effort that an actor playing any one of them for a year would kill the parts, and so kill the plays, or he would kill himself. The box office never dominated Shaw. He swept away the box office as he swept away the stupidities that littered the stage: but there are few playwrights with the fighting abilities of Shaw. We may have his courage, but courage may slay ourselves. Shaw's courage, so well directed, slew all who tried to slay him. O'Neill, if he ever thought of the box office, would never have written *Strange Interlude*, *The Great God Brown*, or *Mourning Becomes Electra*.

No: managers and actors are still terrified of anything new. Tell us the old, old story, say the managers, so that the theatre may be made a place for the box offices to live in! In a programme of a play running recently in the West End, the most important things mentioned are, not the play, not the actors, but a dress designed and made by Messrs Tweedledeedum, and gloves, bags, and silverware designed and made by Messrs

Tweedledumdee. The one thing forgotten on the programme was to mention that the author, the actors, and the audience were designed and made by God Almighty. Long ago, we used to go to see the play; later on we went to see the actors; now we go to see the dresses, negligees, nightgowns, hats, gloves, and silverware. That's the kind of dramatic art we get since the box office has become the guardian angel of the English theatre.

Another sign of the evil effect of the box office: some time ago, in a kind of competition, a London management asked for plays. Before the sun could move from one solstice to another, the management was struggling with 1,600 plays. Just think of it – not 1,600 managements fighting over one play, but one management fighting with 1,600 of them! What was the result? One thousand five hundred and ninety-nine good plays and one bad one? Hardly. Out of this mass of plays there were but two having a possible chance of production. Now this management wasn't one bossing a theatre like the Art Theatre of Moscow, or the Guild Theatre of New York, or the Abbey Theatre of Dublin, all ready to put on second-rate plays, at a pinch, but eager to get plays that would make a name for themselves, at home and abroad. No: the management that dealt with the 1,600 plays wasn't so eager for world-wide fame as it was eager to secure a commercial success. And out of these 1,600 plays this management got two that were possibly fit for production. We may safely assume that the writers of these plays had their eyes fixed fast on the box office. So we see that the box office has a bad effect even on those who concentrate on giving it honour and power. In fact, there are far more failures when the thoughts are of the box office, the whole box office, and nothing but the box office, than when it is completely banished from the mind of him who writes for the theatre.

Look here, Sean, I'm not defending the box office, but are you quite sure that you are thinking clearly? A moment ago you were talking of 1,600 playwrights (yes, it's an awful thought, isn't it!) and you said that only two of them wrote plays that

*were possibly fit for production – good enough to sell to that
management which had organised the competition. But how
do you know that the management selected the two best plays?
If it was half as bad a management as you suggest, it probably
selected the two worst. And how do you know either that all
those 1,600 playwrights had their eyes fixed on the box office?*
Well, mainly because the theatre is so constituted today that it
is next to impossible for anyone writing for it to have his
thoughts anywhere else. What is the art of the theatre today
but a hang-dog attachment to the law of supply and demand?
Give the public what the playwrights and the management
think the public want – that is the law and the prophets in the
theatre of today. The slogan of a great agency is not 'You want
the best plays – we have them,' but, 'You want the best seats –
we have them!' And the law of giving what it is thought the
public want is based on the box office. Only the other day a
playwright who has had a box office success, is reported in a
Sunday paper as saying: 'I think the public taste is for romantic
plays with incidental music, a touch of probability, and characters taken from life.' So, I suppose, we should all strive to write
romantic plays with incidental music till the taste of the public
changes. 'The poets,' says Shelley, 'are the trumpets that call to
battle; they are the unacknowledged legislators of the world.'
Poor Shelley was wrong. Actually, it appears, the poets and
playwrights are but the miserable camp-followers of what is
thought to be the public taste. On the other hand, it may be he
who searches out the public taste who is wrong! He tells us 'he
thinks the public taste is such and such'. He thinks – he doesn't
know. That's the thing that keeps them all hanging by the neck
– the box office is never sure. Well, thank God, it's just as easy
to have a sickening failure with a romantic play tricked out
with incidental music as it is to have a financial failure with a
play by Shakespeare, Shaw, Strindberg, or O'Neill, or any
other dramatist who thinks life is something more than a
romantic glide, helped along by incidental music.

Bravo! I agree with every word you are saying now. Go on, rub it in.

Another sinister attraction of the box office is that when a playwright secures a financial success with any particular play (*The Barretts of Wimpole Street*, for instance), many attempts are made by other playwrights to go and do likewise, and this imitation is encouraged and applauded by the managers on the strength of the idea that what is once done well can be done a dozen times badly. The managers have made imitation the curse of the theatre, as it is, to a greater degree, the curse of the films. How are we to bring about a change? Private energy and enterprise have sprinkled a little theatre here and there in England, occasionally offering a chance of production to a new play by a new dramatist. But even these little theatres are continually struggling with financial difficulties. To do anything they must be nationally and municipally supported. The theatre in Shaftesbury Avenue must become the theatre of Islington, of Fulham, of Stepney, and so on, with the new National Theatre leading the way in greater things for the glory of God and the honour of the English theatre.

I'm not going to let you draw me off your trail with a controversial red herring like the National Theatre. But I am going to suggest that for those ills of our profession today, which you denounce so rightly, the ultimate fault doesn't lie in the managers, nor even in the box office. Surely both fault and remedy lie in ourselves. You've admitted the law of supply and demand. In Elizabethan days England demanded the best from its theatre and got it. Today we – the audience, the people – have grown lax in our demands; we let ourselves be fed with fifth-rate stuff at extravagant prices. But we can still get the best if we want it enough. And, if we want it enough, we'll demand it – and go on demanding it until we get it.

'Tea With Sean', by George Bellak, *Theatre Arts*, September 1953

The tea is strong and plentiful . . . O'Casey fills his pipe content-edly and relaxes on the couch. Breon puts a small cushion just above his father's shoulder, and O'Casey rests his head as he puffs away and talks . . . 'Tis madness to be a playwright . . . First to get a manager to accept the play . . . then the manager must find the money to put the play on . . . then a director must be found, then the right actors, for the wrong actors can ruin it all . . . It goes through so many hands . . . better to write novels and send them in through the mail and be done with it . . . All in the lilting light voice. But meant though. Meant.

Totnes, a lovely village, picturesque? . . . Yes, perhaps . . . but below the loveliness, the rot . . . not only in Totnes but all over . . . the product of neglect and loss of hope . . . behind the pic-turesque, historical front, much misery, squalor . . . He searches to the root, does not let the eye accept.

England? Well, it's America who's the boss now . . . England has had great days and has seen the sun set . . . New, vital lands are the ones to reckon with now . . . America, and Russia and the sleeping giant of China, just now getting up . . . the entire East for that mat-ter . . . And Ireland? Well, the talents leave Ireland to get anywhere.

He receives the Bulletin of the Atomic Scientists . . . the possi-bilites of the atom for peace . . . for doing away with man's drudgery are enormous. He leans forward to emphasize his point . . . If only they will let it be for peace . . . If only the tragedy of war is not visited again upon the world, what tomorrows there could be . . . rivers dammed, weather changed . . . the whole face of the earth altered for the betterment of the human race . . . The cushion falls to the floor. He picks it up and replaces it, and there is silence as we contemplate the possible wonders and look at the blue smoke curling up in front of his face.

His own work? Kermit Bloomgarden* had an option . . . Production in Ireland of anything new? Not likely . . . The church is afraid of true religion . . . everywhere . . . A play of his was based upon the Bible . . . Absolutely Bible . . . But showing the true brotherhood of man . . . Church leaders were horrified, blasphemy . . . But Bernard Shaw wrote back . . . Glad to see you're giving them the authorized version.

Shaw? A great man, of course, with inner meanings ignored in England . . . enjoyed uneasily sometimes and seldom liked . . . disliked, in fact. (How will one talk of O'Casey in fifty years, if not in the same terms, lack of compromise, bitter driving honesty . . . and disliked because of it?)

And questions . . . Questions about the Author's League and the Dramatists Guild . . . Not absurd questions, but bread-and-butter queries . . . contracts, rate of pay . . . The Radio Writers Guild strike . . . O'Casey, the trade-union man, the pick-and-shovel playwright . . . a man to trust on a picket line . . .

Television . . . how is it affecting writers? . . . What are the younger writers writing about? . . . How is political repression of the arts affecting them? . . . He has read a great deal about the Congressional investigating bodies . . . How do people in America feel about them? . . . He himself has had a great deal to do with censorship of one sort or another and well understands the ultimate self-censoring effects these investigations may produce . . . Therein lies a great danger.

The talk purrs on . . . Boulder Dam† and Picasso, the BBC and modern novels, Gaelic and fashions in clothing. The head moves on its cushion. The pipe jabs in emphasis. The voices bound back and forth . . . Suddenly, unaccountably, it is seen that shadows have darkened the corners of the room. The window is no longer a blaze of sun. Reluctantly, the realization comes. The visitors stir about uneasily and rise . . .

---

* Kermit Bloomgarden (1904–76) was a Broadway producer who had notable successes with Lillian Hellman's *Another Part of the Forest* (1940), Arthur Miller's *Death of a Salesman* (1949) and *The Crucible* (1953), and the Goodrich's *The Diary of Anne Frank* (1953).

† Renamed the Hoover Dam in 1947, and situated on the Colorado River, this was completed and opened in 1931, not long before O'Casey's first visit to the United States.

'The Rebel who Never Retired', by Laurence Thompson, *News Chronicle*, 3 March 1955

The taxi-driver, who came from Lancashire, thought that Torquay had recently seen a play by its most distinguished inhabitant, but he wasn't sure.

Mr. Rattigan's Aunt Edna,* who must form a good proportion of Torquay's winter population, would scarcely feel at ease with O'Casey. And O'Casey, in the drawing-room of his airy flat above the town, among the kind of furniture which is pictured in *Homes and Gardens*, and sold by Heal's, seemed little more congruous.

His talk wanders round the firmament, from James Joyce to the Elizabethan English spoken in the Dublin of his youth, from the colour bar to the cobalt bomb, full of crackling phrases – 'You've got to believe in God, if you don't believe in Man' – and self-revealing parentheses – of St Paul, 'I don't give a damn what a man says, or what he believes or what he thinks, as long as he writes well.'

He sees the great world with the disconcerting topsy-turvy wonder of a child: '*The Times*, now, that must be a pretty important newspaper'; and, 'You're from London? There must be an awful lot of London men in the world; the birth rate of that city must be tremendous.'

Surprisingly, after the petty prickliness of *Sunset and Evening Star*, he is tolerant: 'Poor old Churchill, he doesn't seem very hopeful. He sees Russia as the enemy. I suppose it's the only possible view to take from his point of view.'

And looking back to the troubled times without which there would have been no *Plough and the Stars*, he salutes the English as chivalrous, if often stupid opponents: 'The Tommies were always welcome when they came to search. One came to search my room. When he was out of sight of his officer, he let his rifle butt fall on the ground, lit a cigarette and said' –

---

* The playwright Terence Rattigan invented the figure of 'Aunt Edna' to represent the typical middle-class theatre-goer.

O'Casey imitates, not quite correctly, the Cockney whine; he has never been entirely at his ease outside Ireland – '"You haven't anything in here, have you?"

'It was damn cold that winter. Before he sent me outside, the officer said, "Haven't you got an overcoat? You'd better put it on then." He needn't have done that, you know.'

O'Casey insists that he is a Communist. 'But I'm not a Communist pamphlet. There are a whole lot running around who are no more than Communist pamphlets.'

And Soviet art is dry-as-dust, out-of-date. 'I tell them, "You honour Tolstoy and Chekhov, but you'll never have another if you don't be brave."' He recalls how, when Stalin died, Picasso did a child's vision of the dead hero for a French paper, which some bureaucrat condemned. The long, sensitive forefinger stabs the air, and the voice becomes more astringently, defiantly Dublin: 'If I'd been editor of that paper, I'd have written to that Soviet official and said, "Go to HELL!"'

Then a little later there is a parenthesis – 'Anarchism is a higher form than Communism' – and a statement of faith, 'I'm against any system which doesn't allow every man and every woman the admission to all the gifts of the universe.' That, really, is what the plays have been about. That is why it is right to call O'Casey, the agnostic, a religious man, and *The Bishop's Bonfire* a religious play.

'It's the spirit of a book written by our own Catholic clergymen, Dr. Walter McDonald, who was forty years a professor of theology at Maynooth.* He wanted theology to advance like any other science. I hope this play may do something.

'The whole play's symbolical. The critics say that I spoil the last act with melodrama. But the shooting's symbolical. If that hadn't been done, if it had ended with Keelin's man going

---

* McDonald's posthumously published *Reminiscences of a Maynooth Professor* (1925) details his struggles with the conservatism of the Catholic church. David Krause describes McDonald as 'One of O'Casey's "martyred" heroes.' (*Sean O'Casey: The Man and His Work*, London: MacGibbon and Kee, 1960, p. 25)

away, that would have meant death, just the same, a life of frustration and despair.'

And that, to the old revolutionary, is a symbol of Ireland, the world. Besides – the Old Micky peeps slyly out – 'I'm still interested in melodrama. I don't see why there shouldn't be a little bit of melodrama. It's a play, you see, the theatre's make-believe.'

Will London see the latest play of the greatest playwright writing in English? He awaits news. London has not been over kind to him. Ninety-nine per cent of his income is from America, and that from the autobiographies rather than plays.

'They've sold not well, you know, but they've kept me from penury. I keep a family of six, you know, and everything's sliced by 9s. in the pound. But I've no reason to complain. If I didn't work, what the hell would I do? I'm a naturally lazy fellow.'

Best of all, perhaps, would be if his own country honoured its own prophet.

'My nearer love is with the Irish people.' A pause and the quick, thin smile that is never far from his lips. 'But they don't seem to appreciate me very much.'

'O'Casey Out to Make Them Laugh', by Donal Foley, *Irish Press*, 13 September 1957

Sean O'Casey was at work on his new play when I spoke to him at his Torquay home today. He was as vigorous, as pungent and as witty as ever in his views. He has changed the name of his new play, *The Night is Whispering*, to *The Drums of Father Ned*. It is a comedy. 'There is absolutely no tragedy in it,' he said, 'I hope it will make people laugh.'

The play is written to the background of An Tostal, which incidentally is one of the Irish activities of which the 78-year-old playwright highly approves. 'I am all for festivities and for any attempt to put Ireland on the map – the Wexford Festival is a right good idea too,' he told me. Like all O'Casey's work, the play, although it promises to be richly comic, will have a serious undercurrent.

O'Casey is also 'jotting down words' as he puts it for a future book, but it has not taken shape yet. The play is taking up most of his time. However, he finds time to look occasionally at television. He saw the TV productions of his own plays and didn't like them very much. He has refused permission to have two of his other plays televised.

His objection to television as a medium for drama is based on artistic rather than personal reasons. He explains the TV does not convey the spirit of a play. And also, the play is often cut drastically in order to fit a given time limit.

O'Casey's health is now much improved. He was in excellent spirits and his conversation ranged from drama to politics and as usual to Irish emigration about which he is deeply concerned. He was immensely pleased about Mr. Aiken's speech at the United Nations.*

Any suggestion to withdraw troops will have O'Casey's approval. The plough is much more important than the gun, he told me in his rich undefiled Dublin tones . . .

'O'Casey, 78, Says Hurrah to Life', an interview conducted over the phone by Don Ross, *New York Herald Tribune*, 16 November 1958

ROSS: *Mr O'Casey, this is Don Ross. I wanted to find out if you are still saying hurrah to life, as you were when you wrote your autobiography.*

O'CASEY: Oh, yes, of course I am. Not so loudly as I did when I was younger, but just as earnestly. My voice isn't quite as vociferous as it used to be, but that's due to years, rather than to any lessening of my desire for life. Isn't everybody hurrahing for life? What are we going to do without it?

That's a very good question. Mr O'Casey, you've been called, as

* Frank Aiken (1898–1983) was the Republic of Ireland's Minister for External Affairs 1951–4 and 1957–69. During this second term of office he greatly strengthened Ireland's position in the United Nations.

you know, the most magnificent prose writer of the English language.
No, I don't think so.

You don't agree with this?
You have one of the finest prose writers that ever lived – that is, in your own country – Emerson – Waldo Emerson and Thoreau – Henry Thoreau. If I'm half as good as either of them, I'll do.

You've been called the greatest living playwright in the English language.
I've been called a hell of a lot of things besides that. That's a very pleasant thing to be called, but I've also been called a lot of unpleasant things.

Like what?
Well, blasphemer, indecent writer, lascivious scoundrel, all sorts of pleasant things like that. I've been called a very bad playwright. It's been said that I amn't a playwright at all.

Mr O'Casey, I've heard it said that among the contemporary English playwrights the only ones who were better than you were Shaw and O'Neill. What do you think about that?
Better than I am? Well, I wouldn't deny it for a moment.

Then you believe it's true?
I don't know whether anything is true or not. But it's my personal belief that it's true. Bernard Shaw was an extraordinarily great playwright and an extraordinarily fine man in every sense of the word. And I think Eugene O'Neill was the same. I always had a profound regard and affection and love for Eugene O'Neill. I knew him personally. Eugene O'Neill was a very, very great man. And a great dramatist. And I don't think you can say anything more than that. He ranks with the great dramatists of the world – Aeschylus, Euripides, Sophocles, Shakespeare, Marlowe and all the Elizabethans, the first-class Restoration writers, Oliver Goldsmith, Sheridan. It's a long list. He belongs to what we call – what Shaw called – 'the apostolic

succession of literature' that goes back many, many years, longer than any church.

Mr O'Casey, are you in the apostolic succession?
I hope I am, I try to be.

As you know, Juno and the Paycock *will be a musical comedy, and, as you know, Miss Crawford and Mr Shenker are producing* The Shadow of a Gunman,* *and* Cock-a-Doodle Dandy *is staged off Broadway, and so on – this is a great revival of interest in your work. What do you think is causing this?*
Well, I don't know, I couldn't say. I can merely guess that it's probably because there are a great many people in the United States who like me. I presume that they like what I've written, and I'm very glad that they do. I have no false modesty about that.

I've been told that you get most of your royalties from the United States.
Yes, I've said that lots of times. I still get most of my royalties from the United States. I don't see why I should hesitate to say that, because it's a fact, and I'm never afraid of facts, I don't like them sometimes.

But you're never afraid of them.
What's the use of being afraid of the facts? You must face them sooner or later, mustn't you? I get most of my royalties – I get my living, that's the way to put it. Royalties is a very *haughty* word, a very professional word. What actually happened is, for many years I've got my living – that's a more living word, actually, 'living' is a more lively word than royalties. I got my living from my *friends* in the United States. Because all that go to my plays and like them must be in one way or another friends of mine, mustn't they?

---

* Cheryl Crawford and Joel Shenker were behind the Actors' Studio production of the play in 1959.

Isn't there something rather strange about a former Irish revolutionary like you coming to rest in England?
Something strange?

Isn't there?
Then you mean that instead of going to England I should have gone to the United States? Most of the Irish revolutionaries used to go of course. But that was the time when England was at war with Ireland. When I came over, England had ceased to be at war with Ireland. Now what do you mean by strange?

Well, here you are, a person who fought against England for a number of years. You were a revolutionary . . .
Not against England.

Well, against English soldiers.
Against the English government. The English government that meant to rule, and that they didn't understand and didn't want. I've always been against colonialism. I'm against French imperialism.

Do you think that this play of yours, The Shadow of a Gunman, *has got anything to say to us today about politics? Is there a contemporary meaning?*
Well, so they tell me . . . they tell me that it's philosophy rather than politics. I don't think there are any politics in the play – that is, current politics. But it's philosophy, general philosophy.

What's the philosophy of the play?
Well, I think the general philosophy of the play is the bewilderment and horror at one section of the community trying to murder and kill the other. Against war, against strife. My philosophy is – speaking directly now – that life, life ought to be a safe thing to live. It oughtn't to be dangerous to live life, ought it? I think that all our efforts should be concerned with making life safe, not making it dangerous. That's why I'm against the hydrogen and all these atomic bombs, and against war. I think they're making life dangerous instead of making life safe.

That's my philosophy, and I think that's the philosophy that's in *The Shadow of a Gunman*.

Why didn't you come to the United States for this gala O'Casey year?
Well, I'm a few months from seventy-nine. I've had seventy-nine strenuous years, and it's taken quite a bit out of me. The soul remains hale, the spirit remains strong, but the flesh is a little weak, you know. And I don't think I'd be able to withstand the generosity of the American people. Don't mind that, because I love the American people, but I must say that the generosity of the American people is dangerous.

When was the last time you were in New York, Mr O'Casey?
I can't exactly say the year . . . it was the year 1934 or '33.

Did you like it?
Oh of course I liked it. The only complaint I had to make was that I had to get out of it . . .

You had to get out of it? It sounds as though the sheriff might have been after you.
Well, my time was up, you know. I couldn't stay for ever. Which was a great pity. I learned a lot from the American people, I learned a lot from their behaviour, the way they spoke, the way they went about, their buildings.

I want to get back to The Shadow of a Gunman *for a moment. I've heard it said that in your plays, it's the women who turn out to be the courageous ones.*
Women must be more courageous than the men. Courage doesn't consist in just firing a pistol and killing somebody else, or taking the risk of another firing a pistol and killing you. I wouldn't call that courage at all, I'd call it stupidity.

What does a woman's courage consist in?
Fortitude – and patience – and understanding.

Is this true, then, that you think that women are more courageous than men?
In life, yes. They're much more near to the earth than men are. Men are more idealistic, stupidly idealistic. They're not as realistic as the women. The woman has to be nearer the earth than the man.

You like women then?
Oh, I like men too, provided they're not bores. But after all, women are half the population of the world – they're very important. What on earth would we do without them? [Laughter] I couldn't live in a house where there wasn't a woman.

How is your wife, incidentally?
Splendid. I like a pretty woman better than an ugly one. You remember what Emerson said about women. A woman that had a charming figure was very attractive, a woman that had a pretty face was very attractive, but that a woman with a pretty figure was more attractive, and that a woman that had a very charming nature was the most attractive of all, but when you put those three things together they make a very beautiful God's creation, don't they?

Did Emerson talk about women? I didn't know he was interested.
Waldo Emerson was interested in everything. Rivers and mountains, and pots and pans, and great revolutions, and the antiquities of Greece and Rome. He was interested in everything that life showed him.

*As a writer who is interested in freedom for writers, do you have any comment to make on the fact that Boris Pasternak, the Russian . . .**

* Boris Pasternak (1890–1960) was awarded the Nobel Prize for Literature in October 1958 but turned it down after being threatened with expulsion from the Soviet Union.

I wouldn't have any comment on that over the telephone . . . The only comment that I would make is this: that from what I know and from what I feel, I think it was a mistake to expel Pasternak. But I believe myself that the donation of the Nobel Prize had a political basis . . . it was due to a political cause . . . it was given to him for a wrong reason . . . it wasn't given to him that he was a great poet, but for political reasons. For instance, what makes me very bitter about this sort of thing is that there's no comment when other writers in other countries are persecuted. There was no one persecuted like James Joyce . . . there wasn't a voice raised to help him. Why didn't James Joyce get the Nobel Prize? He was probably one of the greatest writers in centuries. Yet the persecution of the man was appalling.

Have you read Pasternak's book?
No I haven't. I couldn't. I don't know Russian.

It's been published in English translation, you know.
But I don't trust the English translation. I've read translations of my own. It's not anything, not anything like the original. All the spice and vigour, and revolution and Rabelaisian comedy in the original, they're all gone from the translation. It's a sad thing, this. I don't see why there should be these disputes about literature. I don't think they're necessary. I've never yet met a group of people that would hold the same opinion about a work of literature. You don't expect it. I've been condemned thousands of times in my own country for what I've written. And I can't help it. I think every artist should have freedom. Wasn't it Shakespeare that compared the poet with the lunatic? Every poet and every first-class artist they called a lunatic. Bernard Shaw, and Euripides, and Aeschylus and Shakespeare and all these men were close to lunacy.

Close to it, eh?
Close to it insofar as the curious visions they saw, the tremendous amount of evidence that they could throw out in front of

them. They could see as many extraordinary things as any lunatic . . . or any lover. The lover, the lunatic and the poet, they all see the same thing. 'More devils that vast hell can hold,' on the one hand, and the lover seeing, 'Helen's beauty in the brow of Egypt.' I don't see why the artist shouldn't have the same liberty as the lover and the lunatic.

You're for freedom for the artist.
Of course I am. I always have been.

But here is a situation in the Soviet Union where they have forced Pasternak to reject the Nobel Prize. Is this freedom?
Well, of course, that's their business, not mine. I was banned recently in Dublin, myself. Only recently they wouldn't let a play of mine go on in Dublin. So you see, I know what it is. I experienced it.

Which one of your plays do you think was the most successful? Which one do you like the best?
Which way? You mean financially? As a drama?

Which one in your opinion was the best play?
My favorite's not necessarily the right one. If you want to know my favorite play, it's *Cock-a-Doodle Dandy*. I think that's the most cockeyed, and it's a ball from start to finish. It's by far the best I've written. That's my opinion.

Look, I've always been curious as to why you call yourself 'the green crow.'
Well, I have great admiration for the crow. I always have had admiration for that particular bird. It's supposed to be the most intelligent bird in existence. The crow. More intelligent than most birds. All birds, practically. It's more a matter of degree. Although I don't look on myself as more intelligent than any other human being. I'm quite convinced that I have my share. Green, of course, is the national color for Ireland. And there was a notice – a criticism of a recording of mine on a gramophone record – said of my voice, 'very interesting and fascinating, but

as raucous as the cry of a crow.' So I thought it would be a good thing to call a book of essays, 'The caw of the green crow.' And I have a raucous voice at that. It's getting old and hoarse.

Mr O'Casey, thank you.
Well, I hope you're not bored. I'm quite satisfied.

'An Evening with O'Casey', by Saros Cowasjee,* *Irish Times*, 25 July 1959

I rang the door-bell a little after four.

Mrs O'Casey answered the bell. 'Come right in,' she said, leading me into a lovely drawing-room. 'Sean will be here soon.'

O'Casey entered, took me by the hand and led me to the sofa. I kept staring at him . . . Could this old man of seventy-nine be the same Johnny Casside I had read of: a young collar-less labourer given to fierce resentment of all that was mean and sordid, a mad visionary dedicating himself to every progressive movement that held a gleam of hope for suffering humanity: a poor, self-educated Protestant young man who starved himself so as to save sixpences to buy himself books: one who fought against every obstacle that came in his path with a determination to survive and become a great dramatist?

My doubts were brushed aside as he made me talk about the place I had come from and what I was doing. But I hadn't come 250 miles to talk about myself. Soon I was shooting questions at him about his plays. Ah, but he wasn't interested in them. 'What are they but a handful of dust?' he said; 'they are not worth anything.' I could not contradict him. I could not tell him that back in Leeds I had opened *Roget's Thesaurus* in search of synonyms for epithets like 'magnificent', 'excellent', that I had used so often that I now needed some fresh ones.

* Saros Cowasjee was at this time researching a PhD on O'Casey at the University of Leeds. He published *Sean O'Casey: The Man Behind the Plays* in 1963.

Seeing that he was not anxious to talk about his plays, I turned the topic to Dublin.

'When will Dublin have permission to perform your plays?'

'Not till it produces those plays that were turned down by the Tostal Committee.'

'Do you still love Dublin?'

'Why yes, I love the whole of Ireland, I don't differentiate between the North and the South.'

There was an uneasy silence. I scratched my head for another question. God! Was that all that I had to ask on Dublin? But O'Casey had a question this time. He leaned forward and with mischief in his eyes said to me:

'Tell me, you're not Irish?'

'No, yes – I am not Irish,' I said.

'You seem very interested in Ireland.'

'The Irish have a lust for life, and that draws me.'

He leaned back on the sofa and sadly shook his head. 'That Ireland is gone,' he said, 'that Ireland is gone.' I stared at him. I could see his mind swim back to the agitated Dublin of his youth, and himself in the front of every fray.

O'Casey shook himself up. 'Tell me something about India . . . about Nehru. I have great admiration for Nehru.'

'So have I, but . . . but will Dublin . . .'

'Oh, talk to me about India. Who is the next man after Nehru?'

'I don't know, Nehru doesn't know it either!' I replied.

'I never met Nehru, but Shaw did. But I saw Mahatma Gandhi and even heard him speak . . . a great man, a saint, a great saint. Mind you, Gandhi was a pacifist, while I am not . . . I believe in fighting for my rights. I heard Gandhi once, long back in London. There was a meeting and Gandhi stood on a low platform dressed in his loin-cloth, hand-woven, what do you call it? . . . "khaddar" . . . Khaddar, I get it now. After he had done his bit of speaking, a fellow stretched on a seat in the front row bawled at Gandhi: "Now will you tell me what is a mahatma?" Gandhi looked at him, smiled, and said slowly and deliberately, "A mahatma, sir, is a most insignificant person."'

I liked the way O'Casey narrated the incident in his soft, nasal voice. And as he enjoyed it as much as I did, I made him repeat the whole thing again. From India we drifted to China and Russia. He didn't think that the recent happenings in China and Tibet meant much, nor did he feel that India was in any way involved in this trouble.* 'Communism is out to abolish poverty,' he said, 'we must do away with it. I hate the poor, or nothing can be done to help them . . . we must do away with the poor by abolishing poverty.'

He talked of Communism and what it meant to the world. 'Communists have always hated war; so do all sane men. I never lost my Communism – it merely changed by growing deeper and certain within me.'

'If you were always a Communist, how is it that you did not glorify them in your earlier plays, as you have done in *The Star Turns Red*?'

O'Casey gave me a significant reply, whether we agree with it or not. 'Communists,' he said, 'have glorified themselves more effectively in the world than they have in plays or novels. Besides there is no Communistic dogma in *The Star Turns Red*. It is as Shaw saw – the spirit and prophecy of the Authorised Version of the English Bible.'

He talked affectionately of America . . . said that ninety per cent of his income came from the United States. 'They have a lot of money, must say that they have done a lot of good too . . . but they could do more, more with the amount of money they have. Recently I was offered $2,500 for an article of 2,000 words. God! I needed the money but I didn't like the paper – I refused.'

'But why?' I exclaimed.

'Why? Why should they pay an old man like me that sum for a small article? Why not give a chance to a young and struggling writer?'

His Communism is not a political dogma; it owes nothing to Russia. 'Russia is not Communist,' he told me, 'it will take

* The Dalai Lama had recently fled Tibet after the Chinese invasion.

another sixty years before it goes Communist. Your India may take as much as 150 years.'

. . . Here are some of his assertions:

'I like all my plays; *Cock-a-doodle Dandy* is my favourite though *The Plough and the Stars* is my best play.

'I enjoy thinking and planning out my plays, but hate writing.

'I am not anti-Catholic. I only attack some of its practices which I think to be wrong.

'All my characters in all my plays are taken from real life. I knew Captain Boyle very well . . . a splendid drunkard, but a rotten husband.

'Yeats was the greatest poet of our age. A little vain and proud at times, but there was some justification for it.

'Nietzsche is out of date: Schopenhauer is too pessimistic.'

He had some advice for me.

'Don't waste your time in the British Museum or in any other library. There are many better things that you can do.

'Forget your work. What difference will it make whether you succeed or fail? The more important thing in life is to live.'

'Figure in the Shadows', by W. J. Wetherby, *Guardian*, 10 September 1959

The strong young voice on the telephone I supposed to belong to Sean O'Casey's son. He had the impish tone of an irreverent son when he asked why on earth I wanted to see old O'Casey. He led me on to reply a little indignantly that, like many other people, I thought O'Casey a great dramatist, strangely neglected at a time when the English theatre possessed talent but no other recognisable genius. 'Many other people, indeed!' said the voice. 'You and not many others in England. It's fifteen years since O'Casey had a play produced in London.' Then, in an off-hand way, he added: 'And this is O'Casey speaking.'

So much used to be made of his famous fighting spirit, of his sympathy for the underdogs and his belief in communism as their salvation, that the impression remains of an embittered Don Quixote tilting at everything and everybody within reach, as if he has been neglected simply because those who could have helped had to withdraw to a safe distance. Nothing could be less true of the man. At eighty 'or as near as damn it', he has something of the serenity of the elder Bernard Shaw and the life-love of an old 'warrior', as he once called Yeats; a warrior who has fought his way through life to wisdom.

Show in conversation the red rags of his legend – politics, religion, some of the Irish clergy's attitude to his plays – and he does not charge, but, with a steely twinkle glinting through his spectacles merely makes you feel deceived by what others have said about him. He once told Mrs Bernard Shaw, who was worried about his reputation as an Angry Young Man, 'I assure you, I shrink from battle, and never advance into a fight unless I am driven into it.' He still has an exhuberant love of life – 'If only an eightieth birthday meant you could be ten years younger,' he told me – and often when he has been 'driven' into a fight, the cause has been the memory or fear of life being wasted. The searing poverty he saw in Dublin as a boy impressed on him how youth could be thrown away. A key passage in his plays is the description of Mrs Boyle in *Juno and the Paycock* in which he comments about her life of anxiety in the working class: 'Were circumstances favourable she would probably be a handsome, active, and clever woman.' This explains the moving way in which today he talks of youth, and his efforts to help to make sure it is not wasted in all the countries he knows. Those who make so much of his enthusiasm for Soviet Russia also forget his long love-affair with the United States (which is least guilty of neglecting him) and that he chose to live in England, whose ordinary people he is quick to praise.

I asked him whether bitter memories did not make him overrate communism as a panacea. He did not think so. The young people in Russia decided what they wanted to do, he said, and they all got jobs. 'I understand in England that many young people leaving school cannot get jobs at once and are unemployed.

That's a terrible thing.' Did he exaggerate? 'I hope I do,' he replied. 'Oh, I hope I do.' He did not seem concerned about political systems so much as the young people themselves. That was the real O'Casey talking.

In a typewriter in his workroom was a half-completed page of a new play, *Figuro in the Night*. He had already completed another new play, *Behind the Green Curtains*. Both had 'a kind of fantasy like life itself', but when I asked when they would be produced he answered shortly: 'God knows.'

He began his career with tragic works of realism and then tried to expand the range of the contemporary play with combinations of realism, fantasy, dialogue and song. To judge by the fashionable experiments in this style of the Theatre Workshop Company in the West End, Sean O'Casey was at least twenty years ahead of his time.*

Mrs O'Casey had been to see the production of *Cock-a-Doodle Dandy* at Newcastle-upon-Tyne on its way to the Edinburgh Festival and then London. His admirers will hope that this production in London shortly will mark the start of a great revival of his plays during his eightieth year. The revival seems bound to come eventually, and it would be tragic if it came only after he was no longer here to enjoy it. He often thinks in dialogue, he told me, and so here are some of his 'thoughts' to me:

WETHERBY: *You were once quoted as saying you were an exile from everything.*

O'CASEY: I never accept anything that has not my name to it because many things have been said about me that are not true. I have never been exiled from life and that is the only thing that matters. I'll be exiled enough when I go off at the end from all the things I love and participate in. Most of the modern writers

---

* Theatre Workshop, founded by Joan Littlewood and Ewan MacColl, was based from 1953 at the Theatre Royal, Stratford East, and produced politically radical plays, often in agit-prop style. At the time of this interview, their production of Brendan Behan's *The Hostage* (1958) was playing in the West End and seems likely to be the reference point here.

are so god-damn gloomy. They reject life in every concept, yet they cling to it if they get a cold or a fever and rush to the doctor and appeal to him to set them on the road again. You'd think they would welcome the way to the tomb, but they don't. I want to live as long as I'm active and can more or less look after myself and not be a burden or a nuisance to myself. I can't understand how the hell any young man is despairing in life.

What do you think about our ways of preparing people for life?
I'm against any prison system of education in high school, secondary school, or university. Packing with facts to the point of suffocation is an extraordinary way of drawing out a human mind. But I'm not an authority on education. Lots of people make the mistake of thinking when I say something I mean to be positive about it. I just have an opinion like anyone else. Oxford and Cambridge, the king and queen of English universities, have a monopoly of influence and fame they ought not to have. The best of the education that comes out of them is due to the opportunities offered for students to come together and hold discussions.

Do you believe in communism, in politics generally, that power corrupts?
Oh you Liberals are all alike. You always trot out that saying . . .

I'm nearer an anarchist than that.
Anarchism is a high philosophical state. Remember, we must all do our best with what we have. We can't just say 'No' to life. It is regrettably true that every great change has brought upset and suffering, whether it's the Industrial Revolution or communism. Soviet communism as far as I know is a Russian system. It is peculiar to the Russian people. English communism when it comes, as it will eventually, will not be the same at all. An Englishman can't be a Russian any more than you can make an Irishman an Englishman. I saw a Russian come over here to teach drama – a nephew of Chekhov, Michael

Chekhov. He taught the Russian Stanislavsky way of acting.
But it didn't suit the English. They couldn't do it. They looked
laughable when they appeared on the stage. The English must
act his own way, so must the Irish, and the Scot is different
from both. The only similarity is that they speak the same language – a great advantage.

Is the English style no good for your plays?
You can never decide with artists what they can do. An artist
can almost do anything – if he's got genius of course. But the
English as a whole find it difficult to get the Irish lilt and they
put on an accent which is terrible. There are thirty-two accents
in Ireland. Every county has got one. Look how the English
way of speech varies (he did some imitations). The west here is
a very homely and hospitable part, very unspoilt. They're well
away from London. The Home Counties are suffocated by
London manners. I never met the English people until I pene-
trated into the country. When you get away from London, the
English people are truly English. They live their English way
and are very, very charming. But in London, they get spoilt, I
think.

*How long ago is it since a play of yours was produced in
London?*
I don't know. Some time during the war, was it? About fifteen
years.

Why do you think your plays have been so neglected?
(*puzzled*) I don't know. Perhaps as the man said, it is because of
my politics. Or is it that I write bad plays?

MRS O'CASEY: Perhaps they are a bit too good.
O'CASEY: My plays I hope always have a good deal of humour
in them.

*Perhaps what is fashionable to-day is something a little vague,
like Eliot's* The Cocktail Party.
Eliot's integrity is undoubted. I always had a great respect for

him. I reprobated the Soviet Union for attacking Eliot because he's a very honest man. He admits to being an old Tory and a churchman. No one should mind an honest enemy. What you have to be afraid of is a dishonest friend.

What were you aiming at when you changed from the realistic style of Juno?
O'CASEY: I had no aim except to try to write a good play. Nobody lives without a touch of fantasy. I can't stand these little trivial realistic things. The change in my style came spontaneously. I didn't want to restrict the range of the theatre. Neither did Shakespeare. It's not all O'Casey. Shakespeare is full of fantasy, symbolism, song and dance. You would think it's something new. Shakespeare of course is allowed to do it because he is in the English canon. A cult began for realism and it lasted for a while and reached its peak. Nobody could excel the realism of O'Neill.

When O'Neill died, Time *magazine said only Shaw and you outranked him among twentieth-century dramatists.*
That was kind of them. But not *Time* the magazine, but time itself is the only critic which can say whether a man is great or not great. Time discards a hell of a lot of things.

Do you speak your dialogue aloud as you write?
I think in dialogue . . . Realism comes too easy in a way. I think I can create a character and put dialogue into his mouth but I'm not satisfied to do only that.

MRS O'CASEY: It's a pity Sean hasn't had a theatre or a group in which to try out his plays before they were presented to the public.
O'CASEY: I would have liked that. I remember seeing a play of mine acted in the United States and thinking some part of it was underwritten.* Watching the acting, I discovered I had

---

* O'Casey refers here to *Within the Gates*, which he saw performed in New York in 1934.

taken all the leading characters off the stage at the same time. It was not unbearably dull but it was comparatively dull. I rewrote the whole play. If I had had somewhere to run it through, I would have seen that so much sooner. Every town should have a municipal theatre with equal vision from every seat in the house.

Do you miss your connections with the Abbey Theatre?
(*sternly*) I don't think so. I miss the few hundreds a year I had. But I'm told they can't act now. Anyway I've banned my plays in Ireland since that trouble last year over *Drums of Father Ned*. I'm not going to submit any of my plays with the chance of an archbishop speaking against them. Theatre people in Dublin get just a bit jittery when that happens.

Mr O'Casey broke off to search for his tobacco and also showed me a colourful skull-cap, part of his collection of head-gear. He launched into a wonderful story of the old Dublin militia, complete with imitations of the principals. Through the smoke [. . .] he confided: 'You know, if I had my time over again I would not take up writing. It is too precarious. I would take up something like engineering.' But with his talent had he a choice? He replied with feeling, 'I didn't have the choice of being an engineer when I was a boy.'

'O'Casey did not celebrate 80th birthday', *Irish Times*, 31 March 1960

Sean O'Casey, the Irish playwright, who was eighty yesterday, did not celebrate the occasion. 'Why should I? It is just the same as any other day,' he said at his Torquay home. He spent most of the day writing.

'I never have, or never will take any interest in birthdays,' he told me. 'What good will birthdays do anybody? I have no time for this good-will Christian charity business on one day of the year only – it should exist all the year around.'

Mr O'Casey said that he would never return to live in Ireland. 'I couldn't stick it,' he declared. 'Neither could Shaw. I am not anti-Irish – I am very much for the people of Ireland. It is the establishment that I am against.'

Ireland had a future, he declared, but it was with her young people. That was why it depressed him so much to see the young flocking out of the country. 'They will keep on going,' he asserted, 'so long as they are held down as they are. There won't be any future for the young in Ireland until we create a present for them.'

Mr O'Casey said that there was no Irish theatre because people in Ireland were too much afraid of offending. This was due to the fact that they had no conception of the Catholic faith. The faith embraced the whole company of the faithful, laymen as well as clergy. It was not confined to bishops. 'The Pope is said to have the key to Heaven,' he added, 'but it seems to me that every Irish bishop has a master key.'

Mr O'Casey declared that one of the great tragedies of the Irish emigration was that it was the young and vigorous who were leaving. There was a danger that eventually Ireland would become almost depopulated in the end. The Government should consider the problem.

'London Letter: O'Casey Speaks', *Irish Times*, 3 March 1962

'Why shouldn't Ireland get into the Soviet bloc? She'd be more secure there.' The trenchancy of the remark will leave no doubt who made it. When I spoke to Sean O'Casey this morning at his home in Torquay, Devon, it was obvious that, in spite of an illness that has lasted eight weeks, his mind has lost none of its liveliness. 'I am not an angel yet,' he said, and went on to show that he is keeping very much in touch with this world by talking about Ireland's application to join the Common Market.*

* Ireland had applied to join the European Economic Community the previous year and was finally admitted in 1972.

The idea that Ireland might go into NATO obviously appalled him.* 'But Ireland has been changing a lot and you'll be pushed in. I can't understand why you don't set up an embassy or a *chargé d'affaires* with the Soviet Union which was the first country to recognise the Republic. It is stupid to ignore her and you could get a good market for your bacon and butter there . . .'

As for writing, he told me that he did not tell people what he was doing. 'I am trying to write,' he told me, 'but I spend a lot of the day reading the *Irish Times*, *Focus*, the *Daily Worker*, and various Soviet and Chinese magazines and newspapers. And I spend quite a lot of time answering letters.'

Asked whether he intended to go to Ireland, he said, 'I'll never go to Ireland again. At eighty-two one doesn't care to travel. But some day the oul' soul might fly to Leinster House to have a look at the Dail.'† I told him that his soul would probably find it depressing. 'What do you mean?' he said. 'Have you never been in the House of Commons?' But it was clear that the chief thing he was thinking about was blocs and divisions between people. 'It is nonsense to talk about this bloc, and that bloc, and the other. Everyone will have to get together some time.'

I mentioned Elizabeth Coxhead's book about Lady Gregory, and he said that he had heard she was now writing one about Maud Gonne.‡ 'But why doesn't somebody Irish write about these people? Are they all envious of what they did?' He said that he had no intention of allowing a play of his to be put on at the Abbey. 'The Abbey died when Yeats died,' he said. 'The standard of acting and production are ruined, and everything you see there now is rubbish. The last time I was in the Abbey was in 1934, when I was in Dublin with my wife, and we saw [George Bernard Shaw's] *Candida*. But they don't produce

* In 1949 Ireland refused to join NATO while still partitioned.
† The Dail is the Irish Parliament.
‡ Elizabeth Coxhead's *Lady Gregory: A Literary Portrait* appeared in 1961. In 1962, Gregory's *Selected Plays*, edited by Coxhead and with a foreword by O'Casey, was published.

plays there any more.' Listening to the crusty Dublin voice, it was evident that however long O'Casey has been in Devon, he has never lost his love for and interest in Ireland.

'The Sting and the Twinkle', by W. J. Wetherby, *Guardian*, 15 August 1962

'Sean is resting. He will be up presently,' said Mrs O'Casey, the beautiful Eileen, the heroine of his work . . . With them at present is his American biographer, Dr David Krause, who is preparing a collection of O'Casey letters which may stretch into three volumes by the time he has run them to earth in several countries.* Soon the prolific letter writer himself appeared. Outwardly there was no change since I last saw him two years ago . . .

'There has been a change,' he said, taking off his glasses. 'My eyes have almost gone now. The most aggravating thing is I can't read in bed when I'm ill and that's terrible because I hate bed. Still I've had them for eighty-three years and they were pretty bad when I was five years of age. I'm not whining about it. It's just that I'm passionately fond of reading. I'm planning to buy records of Shakespeare's plays so if I can't read them I can hear them.' . . .

'You know Yeats didn't have a five-pound note till he was over forty. He told me that himself,' said Mr O'Casey, settling himself at the dining table after dipping his head close to the bowl of flowers near his plate. 'The only hope for the young Irish writers since this bloody England let after persecuting and torturing and hanging us – the only thing for them is to go to that blasted country which persecuted them!'

'You mean the English ruling class of the time persecuted the Irish –'

The bright eyes peered over the table. 'Are you a Socialist by any chance? There's always a ruling class. I had a strong dislike of the English people because I thought them all scoundrels until

---

* In the end there were four volumes, published between 1975 and 1992.

I met them. They were lads from the Buckinghamshire and Warwickshire Regiment brought over to put down the rebellion – young country lads of seventeen or eighteen terrified of what they were going to do, of the dangers and of the death. I saw they were no different from our lads; they were very kindly except in danger when they shot away at any damn thing. We all looked forward to the Tommies coming because they were kindly. The people in the tenement houses used to make tea for them. It was the Black and Tans we hated – most of them were brutal ruffians, though even some in the auxiliary were fine men.'*

He took off his glasses. 'Do you think Marilyn Monroe would have died if we had had socialism? Who killed Marilyn Monroe – that's a question. That was a tragedy that affected me very much. I hate the idea of Hollywood in which she had to survive. She said she wanted to meet me when she was over here and I wish I had. I would have liked to have talked with her.'

'Perhaps you could have helped her, dear,' said Mrs O'Casey.

'Sometimes someone can help another person. Who knows? It's so easy to be foolish and so hard to be wise. I never knew she had such a hard upbringing – all those foster homes, never a real home.'

'It was incredible that it didn't make her hard and bitter –'

'Oh,' said Mr O'Casey. 'Bitterness is no good to you. You only lose if you're bitter.'

. . . 'You know, when I wrote *Purple Dust*, James Agate rushed into print and called me all kinds of names and said I had stabbed England in the back.† That was an extraordinary thing to say – that the two men in the play represented England, a

---

* The Black and Tans were British ex-servicemen recruited to the Royal Irish Constabulary from early 1920 to strengthen the force against the IRA. The name derived from their khaki trousers and dark jackets. They were supplemented by the Auxilliary division of the RIC and both had a well-deserved reputation for brutality.

† James Agate (1877–1947) was drama critic of the *Sunday Times* from 1923. He was disapproving of the kind of theatrical innovation practised by O'Casey.

country of fifty million people, the miners, the dockers, the rail-waymen, the clerical union, teachers, doctors – they're all England. Agate was a bit out of touch – like Asquith with whom I once dined.'*

'Did you write Asquith any letters?' inquired Dr Krause.

'No, he wasn't my kind of man. Very nice. A classical scholar. But out of touch with the life of the people.'

He took his glasses off again. 'I haven't lifted the ban on my plays in Ireland. Except for Bernard Miles – he can take the festival plays there if he wants to.† A kind of hail and farewell. The ban anyway can only apply to professional productions because thirty-five years ago I was very poor and had to sell my amateur rights for a lump sum. But there will be no professional productions otherwise. I'm still very bitter about their failure to stand up against that Roman Catholic Archbishop who didn't like my play . . .'

'Are you in favour of the national theatre?'

'Of course. England ought to have one. There's hardly a country in the world that hasn't – but I'm really much more in favour of municipal theatre. Every town with over 15,000 people should have one. Sir Laurence Olivier ought to be a good director. It's a glorious way for him to end his life.'

'He's only about fifty-five,' said Mrs O'Casey.

'Thirty years isn't a long time to be in charge of a national theatre. There are so many things to be done. That would make him eighty-five, even older than I am. I hope it won't be confined to the Elizabethans. It must be very different from Stratford. It should have room for all the continentals – plays from all the countries of the world.'

---

* H. H. Asquith (1852–1928) was Liberal Prime Minister 1908–16. He introduced the Home Rule Bill in 1916 and had a longstanding interest in Irish affairs. It seems likely that O'Casey met him in London in the early 1920s.
† Bernard Miles (1907–91) was Founder of the Mermaid Theatre, London, which staged *Purple Dust*, *Red Roses for Me* and *The Plough and the Stars* as a Sean O'Casey Festival in autumn in 1962.

'Plus a couple of plays of ours, love,' said Mrs O'Casey with a smile.

'I wouldn't have any objection to that. I would like to see Synge done. Then the O'Neill cycle and Thornton Wilder. I would like to see a Negro play there. There are thousands of plays that should be done, but I suppose they will go on the old conventional lines, producing Shakespeare and *Lady Windermere's Fan*.'

He puffed on his pipe and then took off his glasses again. 'Do you believe in life after death?' he asked suddenly. 'I can't. I would like to because I have so many loved ones that are gone and I would like to meet them again. Then there's George Bernard Shaw, Shakespeare and the whole damn lot – you'd never get bored for a thousand years. But I can't believe it. I have tried but I can't. I can't see any evidence that points to it.'

He was lost behind a cloud of smoke and when he emerged again he looked tired – tired enough for his visitors to retire. He put on his glasses again to see us out.

'Critic at Large: Visit with Sean O'Casey', by Brooks Atkinson, *New York Times*, 31 December 1962

In a new book of essays, to be entitled *Under a Coloured Cap*, he will denounce what he regards as W. H. Auden's dismal view of life. 'Life has never been futile for me,' Mr O'Casey observed. 'Of course, there's been a lot of pain in it, but that's a part of it, and I've also enjoyed the fights I have been in.' The manuscript of the new book has just been examined by his publisher's prudent solicitor. A few cautious suggestions have been made. One that Mr O'Casey regrets acceding to is an impertinent sentence in an essay about Kenneth Tynan, drama critic of the *Observer*.

Within the past few years Mr Tynan has had the effrontery to disparage some of O'Casey's work and make at least one factual error. No man to take anything lying down, Mr O'Casey wrote: 'Mr Tynan has a very bad habit of running too fast in front of his own nose.' Mr O'Casey is sorry to lose a phrase he is fond of. But he does not want to distress his publishers who have been loyal to him for almost forty years. 'I guess I'm softening up,' he said with a wry grin.

'A Great "Hurrah" for Life', Jack Levett, *Daily Worker*, 30 March 1964

When a man has reached the age of eighty-four you can expect him to show some detachment from the problems of life.

Expect that from Sean O'Casey and you have a rude shock coming. For this tiny giant of a man still retains the rip-roaring zest for life that rings through everything he has written for the past forty years.

The full flowering of childhood under Socialism is a vision O'Casey still has constantly in mind, and it was of children that he spoke first when I met him at his home in Torquay.

'There's so much humbug talked in this country about children. Look at all this hoohah about the royal baby.*

'Sure, it's entitled to the good things of life – fresh air, good food, freedom to run and play. But so is every other child, and too few of them get it.

'I've no doubt the NSPCC does some good work. But what they really need to do is to tear down all those rows of back-to-back houses that still crush the soul out of anything young.

'And look at the schools. Oh, there are some new ones, I know. But most of them are still dark and dingy prisons.'

The darkness and dirt of the tenement where he was born on March 30 1880 is still vividly remembered by O'Casey, the last of thirteen children born to a poor Protestant family in Catholic Dublin.

. . . 'But let's stop talking about me. I'm not important. What's happening around us in the world is.

'I've more bitterness now about things – the poverty and misery that still exist around us – than I ever had.

* Prince Edward, now the Earl of Wessex, was born on 22 January 1964.

'And I'm more of a Communist than I ever was.

'The newspapers, now, they make me want to spew – rattling on about the sins of the Soviet Union and never a peep about what's wrong here, under their noses.

'Sure, there are deficiencies in the Soviet Union, but they're being put right. And they're nothing to the deep, wide wounds in our own society.'

Sean's friendship for the Soviet Union has remained constant throughout the forty-six turbulent years of its existence.

The future concerns O'Casey now as much as it did in his youth. His last volume of autobiography, *Sunset and Evening Star*, concludes with a great 'Hurrah!' for life – to all it had been, to what it was, to what it would be. And what it will be, for the peoples of the world, is still in O'Casey's mind at the age of eighty-four.

'Sure we'll get Socialism in Britain. Things are changing all over the world – in this country, too.

'It's not so easy for the police to baton down a working-class demonstration and get away with it, as they did with the unemployed during the thirties.

'And look at all the countries already Socialist or on the road to Socialism. Surely we won't be long in following. It has to come.' . . .

'Abbey has been deteriorating for years, says Sean O'Casey', by John Howard, *Irish Times*, 4 July 1964

Sean O'Casey had not read the statement from the Abbey Theatre directors when I spoke to him today and he was not interested in it.* 'There's no need to read it to me,' he said. 'I can guess what they said. They probably said: "How could O'Casey know anything about it?"'

He said that he did not need to see the Abbey production at

* During the Abbey's tour to London, O'Casey had attacked the quality of their production and the Abbey issued a reply in their own defence.

the Aldwych Theatre to give an opinion about it. 'I judge from the world around me. I can see things and understand things and give opinions about things without seeing them. It is a well-known fact for years now that the Abbey has deteriorated. Who is going to say it has not? It has been going on for years.

'Years ago a public protest was made from the audience against the quality of the production and acting in *The Plough and the Stars*. About a week before the Abbey Company went to London a serious article appeared in the monthly magazine *Focus*, and the writer actually suggested that they should be prevented from going because of the inferior quality of the production. Why didn't the Abbey directors exclaim against this article?'

Mr O'Casey went on to say that many visitors to Ireland dropped in to see him when they came to Britain and they all said that the Abbey was a sorry spectacle.

'What the hell does Blythe* know about the drama, anyway?' O'Casey asked. 'He knows nothing about acting or drama. He may be a good manager in a financial sense but he doesn't understand the drama. I have a letter from him in which he condemns himself. He says they weed out a number of plays that have been submitted until they have about ten left. Then they read these again and select two or three which they consider to be the best and they finally select the one they think will fill the house. That is no way for a national theatre to select a play. They neglect what they think would be a better play if they think it would not make money.

'It doesn't matter if I was at the Aldwych or not. They had to get three of the old troupers – Eileen Crowe, May Craig and Eric Gorman – to play three very important parts. Why had they to do that if the quality of the acting in the present company is so fine as Mr Blythe and the other directors make out? If they are producing such fine actors why had they to get a man of over eighty and a woman of seventy or so to take over those parts? Will the directors answer that?'

* Ernest Blythe (1889–1975) was managing director of the Abbey, 1941–67.

O'Casey seemed in great form as we spoke and before finishing he said he would like to tell people to go to the Abbey and judge for themselves.

'One last thing . . . it has not been pleasant to have to say these things about the Abbey. I would love to see the Abbey the finest company in the world. That is my feeling.'

Mr Blythe, when asked about O'Casey's charge that in a letter to the playwright he had said that they eventually chose a play that they thought would fill the house, and therefore chose plays for their money potential, said last night:

'That is entirely wrong. We never reject a play on the basis that it may not make money, when we find that it is a good play. If we think that a play is good we give it a chance whether we feel it would fill the house or not. But we *do* recall plays that have filled the house and we do *not* recall plays that have not. That is a different thing. It would be senseless to recall a play that has proved it will not make money and that the public have rejected. I may add that if there is a good play that we think will not fill the house at its first presentation, we may not put it on immediately, but eventually we *will* put it on.'

A statement issued by the directors of the Abbey Theatre last night said: 'The directors of the Abbey Theatre have read with great interest Mr Sean O'Casey's announcement that they have been dead for years. They would like to assure Mr O'Casey that, as in the case of Mark Twain, the rumour is greatly exaggerated. Dead men tell no tales, not even that of *Juno* or *Plough* or *Gunman*.

'Mr O'Casey's statement that the directors know nothing about acting or the Drama is patently absurd. The long-standing involvement of each of them in various aspects of the work of the Theatre is common knowledge.

'As to Mr O'Casey's reference to the managing director, the point is that his relationship with the board is precisely that of the managing director of any ordinary business establishment, except that the directors of the Abbey Theatre have always taken a bigger share of control of its work than is customary in a commercial concern. In particular, they have always retained control of the two most important functions in the theatre, the acceptance and selection of plays, and the assessment of the producer's casting proposals.

'In spite of differences of opinion with Mr O'Casey, the directors share his enthusiasm for the idea of making the Abbey Theatre the best in the world, and all their efforts are directed towards that end.'

'Last Thoughts from O'Casey', by 'Mandrake' [John Summers], *Sunday Telegraph*, 20 September 1964

As the Hollywood cameras in Ireland rolled towards a Technicolour fade-out on the last rushes of the *Young Cassidy* film last week, the life of John Casey, better known as Sean O'Casey, was itself fading.

Nevertheless, only a few days before his death, the Dublin-born playwright, so long 'on a Devon rock in exile', was ready to receive Mandrake's reporter and talk about his remarkable life-story: 'The screen play of *Young Cassidy* – actually it's 'Young Casside' in my novels – is a life story running up over half a million words by now.'

The screen play was the last work of playwright John Whiting. And the impact of the film on American filmgoers is going to be particularly interesting . . .

'The film shows Young Cassidy growing up from boyhood in Dublin, the way I did . . . Why did I write *Young Casside* in the third person? I just did, that's all. An American feller by the name of Rod Taylor plays the part . . . Michael Redgrave's doing W. B. Yeats.'*

Starting with the time of his very first play, a skit on the St. Lawrence O'Toole Pipers Band and Club (quickly rejected by

* *Young Cassidy*, directed by Jack Cardiff, and featuring Rod Taylor, was released in 1964. The author of the screenplay, John Whiting (1917–63) was also a distinguished author for the stage, whose works included *Saint's Day* (1951), *Marching Song* (1954) and *The Devils* (1961).

the Abbey Theatre) then his novel *I Knock at the Door*, 'and I had to go knocking on the bloody door till the time I was forty-four trying to get a play accepted', up to *Inishfallen, Fare Thee Well*, the film will end with a mighty riot in the Dublin streets, bringing in characters from O'Casey's other play . . . fadeout on the quayside with young Cassidy waving farewell as he sails for England and exile. The End.

'First play I sent to the Abbey got a rejection slip from W. B. Yeats: "Not far from being a good play."

'I was writing plays – or tryin' to – on bits of old paper my friends picked up off the floor in the places they worked. Couldn't afford a bottle of ink, so I boiled old stubs of indelible pencil to make my own ink.'

His fourth attempt, the play *On the Run* – changed to *Shadow of a Gunman* – together with *Juno and the Paycock* saved the Abbey from literal bankruptcy. '*Gunman* grossed £90 at the box office. I got £4. I still had to go tearing up the roads with a pick and shovel.

'I'd changed my name to Sean O'Cathasaigh but now that I was having plays put on I changed it to O'Casey and kept the Sean.'

The full round beauty of Dublin's accent was still O'Casey's that day – he sounded his 't', like Joxer and Captain Boyle, as 'th'.

'In *Juno and the Paycock* that was a real Captain Boyle and that was his real name. Would he have been insulted? He'd never even heard of the play but if he'd seen it he'd have been *proud* and delighted. Because all the people from the Dublin streets I wrote about liked me. Because I was one of them, in all my sinews and to the last breath in me body.

'I'm still writing, you know. Only me eyes . . . I can hardly see now. Last of it'll be I won't be able to see at all. I'll dictate instead . . .

'This Filthy Theatre argument. Ph-auugh! I'm thinking of writing a new play myself.' The wide, humorous Irish mouth twitched, trying to keep the smile in. 'I'll be calling it "The

Bald Prima-Queera".You have to keep up with the times, you know . . .*

'The Theatre of Pessimism they call it? What did the feller say? "The world is an oyster with nothing in it."

'But that's not pessimism.' Sean O'Casey's hand slapped his kneecap. 'That's poet-thry!'

---

* The title of O'Casey's final essay was 'The Bald Primaqueera', a reference to Ionesco's *The Bald Prima Donna*. See Introduction, p. 18.

Interviews with Practitioners

These interviews, conducted by the author with practitioners who have contributed to productions of O'Casey's work, are intended to give an indication of the nature of some recent interpretations of his plays, rather than to provide a performance history. The interviews with Paul Kerryson, John Crowley and Dearbhla Molloy focus on *Juno and the Paycock*, *The Plough and the Stars* and *The Shadow of a Gunman*. Andy Arnold discusses his productions of *Purple Dust* and *Cock-a-Doodle Dandy*, whilst Shivaun O'Casey, Sean O'Casey's daughter, talks about the experience of directing several of his works, including *Behind the Green Curtains* and a number of the one-act plays.

Paul Kerryson

Since becoming artistic director of the Leicester Haymarket in 1992 Paul Kerryson has directed productions of a number of Irish plays, including O'Casey's Dublin Trilogy.

Leicester has a big Asian population and it also has a big Irish population, and these groups need to be taken into account in our programming.

I came here from the Library Theatre in Manchester, seven years ago. I've worked in other theatres including the Chichester Festival Theatre and the Birmingham Repertory Theatre and I've also worked at the Gaiety Theatre and a couple of smaller venues in Ireland. The first play I directed here was *Shadow of a Gunman*, in 1992, in the studio theatre. It was a play I had wanted to do for a long time. There wasn't a history of Irish work being staged here, certainly no O'Casey, which I thought was a great deficiency in the programming, regardless of my own interests. There's nearly always something going on politically which makes that play relevant, and at the time it certainly hit a chord with the critics. It seemed to reflect some of the disruptions that were then going on in Ireland, but then unfortunately it always does. That could perhaps be one of the reasons why O'Casey's plays have lasted; they reflect a long-term struggle.

It's a very intimate play. In the studio theatre the audience felt as if they were in that room with those characters. It was not a well-known play and it has to be extremely well acted. O'Casey's technique is to take the audience in with the comedy, and then the tragedy hits very hard. That's his method of putting a point across. Many other playwrights try to do that but they don't often succeed as well as Sean O'Casey does in mixing humour with tragedy. The danger, of course, in performing the play is that, if you go too far with the humour, the audience won't take in the tragedy, and of course it's vital that they do. That ending comes as a shock, not least because of the innocence involved: Minnie is a total innocent.

All the company members for *Shadow* were Irish, bar one. That's very important for me, and the actors always agree that you have to get performers who can really speak the rhythms of the language. It's very difficult for a non-Irish person to do that. It's not just a question of mimicking an accent; it's all based on something deep in the soul, and it is very difficult, I have to say, for a non-Irish person to get away with it. These plays are written by an author who has witnessed and observed local idiosyncrasies, and those things are very difficult to understand unless you know that culture intimately.

The play had a big cast for a studio production but it was very popular with audiences, and a lot of people here were surprised. I wasn't, though, because I knew it was a good play and that it would appeal not only to the Irish community but more widely as well. We followed it up a couple of years later with

The Plough and the Stars. With that play I decided to go a bit further because *The Plough and the Stars*, in my opinion, doesn't suit a studio setting, because it's an epic play. The action's not just in a room, it's on the streets. This was reflected in the setting; what we chose could almost be described as surrealist. We had a big altar, as a backdrop, and then along the side of the stage was a row of houses, going smaller into the distance, and in front of each one was a cross. This was to symbolize that each household has had its own tragic experiences. Right down at the front of the stage, was a V-shaped wire enclosure and by hanging some pictures on the wire it was made to represent Nora's room. Then for the street scene, the wire was thrown down on the floor over wooden crosses and it became a barrier across the street. For the last scene, in Bessie's attic, we put the wire back up again with a window frame in it so that she could see out into the street, and there was a trap-door in the stage that was used as the entrance.

It was a very strange setting, very different from the way the play is normally done. Certainly at the Abbey, they seem to regard these plays as somehow sacrosanct and would tend not to try anything of that kind. I'm not saying that experimenting with settings is always successful, but one reason I chose to do that was because of the way Sean O'Casey actually went in his own writing. The next play after *The Plough and the Stars* was, of course, *The Silver Tassie*; he himself went into a less realistic mode and I definitely think that the seeds of that were sown in *The Plough and the Stars*. *Juno and the Paycock* is very definitely located in 1922, with the Black-and-Tans in the background, and so is *Shadow*, but I think that despite its historical references, *Plough* is linked to *The Silver Tassie* and O'Casey's exploration of surrealism and expressionism. *Cock-a-Doodle Dandy* is another, even more extreme example of that. I think that he was actually well ahead of his time, even in terms of intimating how things should be staged. Naturalism was simply the predominant style at the time, but now we wouldn't think twice about doing something surrealist or abstract.

I wanted to do *Juno and the Paycock* on the main stage as well, but because of other programming commitments we went back to the studio. For that production, I mixed up naturalistic and non-naturalistic elements. We did have the room, but beyond that was an abstract tapestry, with little houses and hills, and also Mary and the Sacred Heart. Again, because there is only one set in *Juno*, the audience felt very claustrophobic in that room and of course when Jack cooks the sausages, they smell them. That was the sort of effect you couldn't create in a big theatre: we had a real cooker on stage and real sausages, and some nights, just when Jack had a line about the sausages, they would sizzle on cue. The audience responded of course, and they knew it wasn't planned or on tape because they could see the sausages and they could see the spit. Although that's not really an important moment in the play, it was important for us because it made the audience feel, once again, that they were there in that room. When tragedy came into that room, I felt that it was almost unbearable for the audience, in that play to a greater extent than in *Shadow*.

The other important aspect of *Juno*, apart from the political aspect, is what it's saying about women. I think the ending really points this up. The three women have a scene together, and you might think that that's the end of the play, but then Boyle comes in drunk, and collapses on the floor. Some people think the play should end with Juno's 'hearts o' stone' speech, but I totally disagree with that. It misses the point. Having Jack come back on shows what the women have left behind them, and the play is saying that women can survive alone and don't have to have drunken husbands. That was a very brave thing to say at the time he was writing. Women had a particular role in Irish society; the woman's place was definitely at home looking after the men. But O'Casey almost seems to suggest at the end of that play that no matter what disasters befall her, the strength of a woman is that she can start again. All three of them, even Mrs Madigan next door, go out of the room together; the point is that they *leave*. Of course these days people suggest that women will eventually sort out the problems in Ireland because men don't seem to have had much success, that it will be the women who will eventually solve this man's problem of Ireland. And that could come true. There's also a connection here with why Asian audiences like this play because in its representation of the position of women in a patriarchal and religious society, they can see links with the Asian community today.

Do you think audiences have problems understanding the political aspects of these plays?

I think that these days audiences are aware of the general issues; but I do think that many English people were brought up with a very negative image of Ireland. Ireland went through from the thirties to the sixties having to really struggle; it was not a wealthy nation and only in the last ten years has Ireland become, in the English psyche, not only acceptable but desirable. The stereotypes of the Irish as stupid, and all those Irish jokes, seem to have been swept away. Everybody is much more in tune with the Irish problem, as if it's just about what has happened in the last twenty-five years, but at least it's not something that's being brushed under the carpet. I think that there's an understanding, or a willingness to understand, that wasn't there before, and these plays seem even more relevant. You'd perhaps never get *Juno* being done in Leicester in the forties or fifties because the English weren't really interested in the Irish. Now we're having to be interested. These plays come into focus again and they're even more vital now than ever. People want to listen, not just because these are great pieces of writing but because they say something relevant. I think people now consider O'Casey's plays, especially *Juno*, to be among the greatest plays of the century, and quite rightly so. I doubt they'd have said that forty years ago, not in England. Even when these plays were first done in Ireland they were greeted with suspicion. So I think it's only now that they're coming to be appreciated and accepted right across the board.

Did your production of Plough *also stress the religious aspects of the play?*
The religious imagery is inherent in all the plays. It might some-times seem to be treated as a bit of a joke, but when the chips are down nearly everyone's guided by a religious sense. It's ingrained in the culture. Even if you reject it, it still guides you: it guides you in the way you reject things. I don't think it's a decision you make, whether or not to emphasize religion, it's there in nearly every line of the play.

Of course, in *The Plough and the Stars*, you also find the same mix of tragedy and comedy that's there in *Shadow*. The shock comes early on, though, and *Plough* is a real emotional roller coaster. In *Juno* as well, you're in what's almost a parlour comedy for much of the second act, until they're in the middle of the party, drinking and singing, and suddenly Mrs Tancred comes in, totally distraught because they're taking her son's coffin out. Up to that point – and it's a long way into that play – it's all been very amusing. It's a love story with a young cou-ple. You engage with all these characters and you get to know them and see their faults. And then of course the play goes on to make its horrendous point. That little scene affects all their lives and brings everything to a halt. Juno blames herself about Johnny, and that's where God comes in. Towards the very end of the play she says to Mary: 'We'll want all the help we can get from God . . .' I mean everybody from all walks of life and cul-tures can recognize that guilt, and because the play has been constructed with comic elements you can take that tragedy at the end, and I think that's why it is often acknowledged as the best. There are other reasons as well, but if I had to sum it up, that's why. Audiences are very unpredictable. They can be put off within half an hour if they don't like what they're seeing, and I think that although they do like *Plough*, it does seem to be, as I've said, much more of a roller coaster.

When you did Shadow *did you have it in view that you'd even-tually like to do* Juno *and* Plough *as well ?*

Yes. We didn't do them in the order of being written, but I think that was simply because *Juno* wasn't available when I wanted to do it. We nearly did *The Silver Tassie*, but Lynne Parker at the Almeida had taken the wind out of our sails with her production in 1994. With that play, I think there's really only room for one production. She did it very well and I think it's his most daring play. As I mentioned, O'Casey developed into that surrealist mode which I reflected in our production of *Plough*. But *The Silver Tassie* is a very difficult play to stage and I would say that it's a difficult one for the public to get a grip on, at least partly because there's not so much humour in it. I think that's why they've never taken it to their hearts. It's never really had the staying power of *Juno* because, again, people like to be in that living room. If you open up the action, the audience is witnessing and observing rather than being in that room. Perhaps it's something of a generalization, but it seems to me that audiences like being in those rooms. If you're in a room, and there are guns coming through the windows, and you've become involved with those characters, there can be a fantastic atmosphere.

What do you think of Yeats's criticism of The Silver Tassie: *that because O'Casey hadn't actually experienced those things, it wasn't such a strong play, and that he was better at writing about experiences he knew?*
I'd have to call into question a lot of Yeats's judgements, and I don't think I'd go along with that, no. I don't think a writer has to experience something in order to write about it, and in any case Sean O'Casey was around during the First World War, he knew what was going on. He didn't have to be there on the front line. The front line, as *Plough* says, is on your doorstep, like the crosses in our set. I think that some of his more obscure and less realistic plays may also be good, but they don't speak to a modern audience, while the Irish problem is still there, right in front of you. If the Irish problem wasn't still there, I'm not sure that these plays would be staged so often. Whenever

97

they are staged the audience come out saying, 'Oh God it's still going on, why don't we learn, why haven't we learned from all these characters?' They've been saying this for a hundred years. And the play seems fresh, it could have been written yesterday.

So you wouldn't ever be tempted to do any of those later plays?
No. As a director I put these plays on because I was born in Ireland, I come from that stock, and I understand those words and want to share them with an audience. I couldn't say the same about his later work, but that's not intended as a criticism of Sean O'Casey. It's just to do with what I want to achieve as a director. His later plays showed him to be ahead of his time, but I don't think that they have anything in particular to say today. They seem like curiosities. To be honest, for a play-wright to have a legacy of three plays, which are all still per-formed, and are all still significant, is a great achievement.

John Crowley
At the time of this interview in the autumn of 1999, John Crowley's production of *Juno and the Paycock* had just opened at the Donmar Warehouse in London, where he is associate director.

I was a student at UCC in Cork; I did philosophy and English, and then I did a Master's in philosophy and the philosophy of theatre. While I was studying there, I directed student shows, and that's how I started directing. I wasn't really interested in the classics when I was at university; I was far more drawn to new work and devising with actors, the kind of work that peo-ple like Robert Lepage were doing. Then when I left university, I went to the Goodman Theatre in Chicago for five months on a directing scholarship, and while I was there I got a call from Joe Dowling, who had seen one of my student productions which had transferred to Dublin. He had been involved in the selection process for the scholarship, and he was due to revive his production of *Juno and the Paycock*, which he had origi-nally done at the Gate in Dublin in 1986. This was now

1992–3, and I think he mentioned that it was his seventh production of it, or the seventh recast. The production was being put together to tour England with a view to going to the West End, which it duly did.

I had no interest in O'Casey, really, and I suppose I had very little interest in classical Irish drama in general. I did like some of Synge's work, but not plays like *The Playboy of the Western World* – not the classics, or the staple diet of the Abbey, shall we say. I suppose that was largely born out of a degree of cynicism that I had towards Dublin theatre and what I had seen there. I didn't see Joe's original production of *Juno*, but I had seen other O'Casey productions, and I never liked them. I thought it was just slightly sentimental Dublin nonsense, and it didn't attract me on any level. I had studied him a little bit in university, but it's possible to write critical essays and yet never actually capture the power and beauty of a writer.

So Joe very kindly offered me the position of assistant director. Now, he didn't need an assistant director in the sense that he needed somebody to run rehearsals with him, because he had four weeks to rehearse it, and it was very well rehearsed. He knew what he wanted; the production was a very clear template in his head and the actors had to be fitted into it, so to speak, while allowing their own creativity and innovation to work its way into the process as well. Essentially, though, it was the same production he had done before, the set was the same, the costumes were the same, and his reading of the play was the same. My job was to be a caretaker or watchdog as it went around on tour, because it opened in Belfast after four weeks' rehearsal and Joe had to go on to another project and was unavailable to nurture it past opening night. It's quite a hard thing for actors, to have a director for four weeks, technical rehearsal, dress rehearsal, open on a Monday and that's it: it's very rare to not even have previews. So that was my job, to stay with the actors and take the structure that he had set in motion with them, and the journeys he had set them on with their characters, and to keep working with them. I also had to do understudy rehearsals and direct an understudy version of the play based on his production. It was a very interesting exercise and in doing all of that, which lasted for three or four months, I must have seen the play between seventy and a hundred times. I spent a lot of time around it and I did bits and pieces of historical research and research on O'Casey, and that's really where I fell in love with his work.

Was that a good way to begin directing?
I can't really say it was. I mean it was a good experience, but ultimately I think the only way to learn how to direct is to do it, and working with actors is only one part of it . . .

Anyway, after *Juno*, I assisted on various other productions in Dublin, and after a time I had the chance to become a co-director on a production of *The Master Builder* that Brian Cox was staging in Edinburgh. That was an important break for me and afterwards I was offered work back in Dublin, as a director. In the meantime I was also doing my own devised work with the Bickerstaffe Theatre Company in Kilkenny. Then I was invited to come over and do some workshops at the National Theatre Studio, and I came and worked on a Yeats play, *Purgatory*. This led to me being invited by Richard Eyre to direct a show at the National. That was a play called *Fair Ladies at a Game of Poem Cards*, an eighteenth-century *bunraku* play in a new verse translation by Peter Oswald. When I was casting that, Sam Mendes, who'd seen some of my work in Dublin invited me to come and do a show here at the Donmar, so then from that point I stayed in London. I've worked at the National, and I've done four shows here, but in all that time I did want to return to O'Casey, and about two years ago Sam put the idea my way and said, 'What Irish playwrights would you like to do?' He'd previously directed *The Plough and the Stars* and so *Juno* was an ideal one for us to do, and we both knew that Dearbhla Molloy wanted to play the part, so we started from there and began to put the play together.

Were you consciously reacting against that earlier production when you started planning this one?

Yes I was. What was interesting about that production was that Joe took the play from the Abbey, where its history was very deeply rooted and ingrained and where it had become almost vaudeville knockabout, a set of turns for two comic actors, rather than a play which had a very harsh social reality about it. When Joe took it to the Gate, that for a start was quite shocking, because the Gate was regarded as the heart of Anglo-Irish theatre, which is to say that it took care of Restoration work, and Oscar Wilde, and Shaw, and would venture into English work like Coward. Everything about it was associated with the Anglo-Irish upper and middle classes, whereas the Abbey always prided itself on its PQ – what was known as its Peasant Quality. That's not my phrase; it would be used to describe actors. To have PQ would stand in your favour; it meant you were eminently castable. The Gate had never, to my knowledge, done an O'Casey before then. To take the play and put it into that context was something quite shocking in itself and something quite new. Then Joe gave it an edge, in casting Donal McCann as the Captain. Donal had a sort of danger about him as an actor; he was a brilliant comic actor but his Captain certainly had a violent edge to it; there was a latent sense that he wasn't just a buffoon or clown, an old Irish stage stereotype.

I'm conjecturing about the effect this must have had, because Joe also injected a degree of brutality with the Diehards, the Irregulars. In a sense I think he was talking about the current political climate in the North, and he was injecting O'Casey's anti-heroism with an edge which he was then trying to extend to a modern Irish political context. O'Casey is concerned in the play with anti-heroism and its expression in language, and how language can be used to make one set of people shoot another set of people, and I think Joe gave that a political slant. The Mobiliser and the Irregulars came across as being rather more dangerous than they had before. Every generation has to reinvent the play for itself and I toured with that show in large proscenium-arch theatres, and always felt that it would be wonderful to do O'Casey in a really intimate context. So my approach to the piece was immediately in reaction to that production, not necessarily because of Joe's reading of the piece, but in terms of the kind of experience the audience would have.

O'Casey, as we know, was massively influenced by music hall and vaudeville, and also by Ibsen, Shakespeare and Shaw, and nineteenth-century novelists, and it's possible to isolate his dramatic influences and foreground any one of them. For me, the music-hall quality was more to the fore in Joe's production by the time I worked on it, which is to say, the comic aspects. I suppose I wanted to see what it would be like to do it in an intimate space where the comedy would be far more low-key, and where the acting styles demanded by the piece could be almost cinematic, in close-up. That's something that's difficult to do in a larger space because O'Casey writes characters who have a sense of themselves *as* characters: they perform. The Captain performs, Joxer always has a phrase for every word, and Johnny has a layer of performance with his republican cant. Every one of them has a role that they're playing within the world of the play. For me, when that role gets blurred and the volume gets turned up on it, because you're in a big house, and because you're emphasizing a certain sort of comic element, you begin to lose the reality, the fabric of what he writes. Even though it's a harsh world, the fabric of it is quite delicate and is quite easily ripped apart; it can stop being completely real. So by doing it in here, the approach, without wishing to be pretentious, was for it to be almost like an installation in the building.

We started by looking at how we would design it for that space. The design for the production I worked on was pretty close to what O'Casey suggested, with the windows upstage, and Joe had added one extra feature to it: they'd subdivided the room, put a second room in on top, which gave a feeling of claustrophobia. We've given O'Casey what he wants here, which is two rooms, one room stage left, and stage right leads off on to the staircase. But he also specifies two windows upstage centre and there's a convention to do with stage design of the period, that if you have windows upstage centre, you have something on the far side of them – that is to say, a painted backdrop of the street. Rae Smith, the designer, wanted to avoid that illusionist or painterly approach to design, so where to put the windows became a massive problem, and it brought us face to face with the problem of reality, of believability. No matter how believable the acting is, if they're in front of two Georgian windows outside of which is a painted backdrop, in a space this size, I think the audience's experience will always be undercut. We had to find a way round that, because you have to have a window for Joxer to duck out of, and they see the funeral out of it. It was all about how to marry the Donmar space to the demands that O'Casey has written into the play.

We made a choice from the start as well that we were not going to make a design statement with the piece. I think that's quite important because, again, the fabric of what he has written is very much sociologically rooted. You have to have the Georgian room and you have to have the poverty. That's the conceit, not anything else, and if you start fiddling with that, putting in an extra design concept on top of it, you're in trouble. O'Casey's actually a very visual writer and sets the action in a fine drawing room where the English aristocracy would have danced and that has now fallen by the wayside. Then, when the money is dumped on top of that family in Act Two, there's another party in that room, and there's a new respectability. That for me is the visual journey of this play. Somehow, we wanted echoes; the wallpaper's rancid, there's mildew all over the place and the shadow of where there's been a painting on the wall, and those things created the sense of a former life. Part of the floor has been stained from where there was a rug and now there's just bare floorboards. It's like an archaeologist finding traces of a former life. Then, in Act Two with the arrival of the new furniture, you get furniture that is of a cheaper, more vulgar quality, and the new rug doesn't quite fit to the edges. You can't quite restore it to the beauty it had before. Everything on the stage is real, you can touch it, because those characters are completely rounded in an old-fashioned sense. I feel what one has to embrace is the psychological realism of the piece, the 'fourth wall', and in this case we've got two extra walls missing, because the audience are on three sides. You're eavesdropping on that room, you're right in it; it's only three rows of audience deep.

Once you create a room in there, you then have to be very detailed, down to the tattoos on the Captain's arms, down to having no make-up. Every costume has to be perfectly made and they're all authentically done, cut as they would be in the twenties. It puts a vast amount of pressure on every single thing. If you say to an audience, 'Look at this, this is real,' you then can't have a 1990s frying pan, for instance, which we had for the first two previews because we couldn't find the right one. You have to really go the whole hog with the clutter in the room. That's what we went after here, doing it in a cinematic way, to be close and to somehow create the life of it, having the stairs outside the door so that everyone who walked in and out of that room had to walk up stairs. I don't think O'Casey was messing with anything expressionist until much later, until *The Silver Tassie*. He knew exactly what he was doing with the Dublin Trilogy and I think the task is very clear. You have to go after it with a scalpel, go after what he wants with real precision.

So is that a reaction against the production I worked on? I'd say yes, because it was inspired by the context in which we're doing it. Not having to do it in a large proscenium space allows a certain kind of freedom for us in terms of staging it. It brings problems with it, but it means you can do it like you're doing it in a room. Having the audience on three sides means you have to stage it in a very different way. It's much harder to stage something exactly as you would stage it in a room than it is to stage it on a pretty much straight axis in a proscenium arch, so certain stories leap out a lot more. It's a lot darker in this context because you're right up against it, and it means that we've had to tone down certain of his influences. The more vaudeville, comic qualities aren't so much to the fore, and we've had to handle the melodrama of Johnny's story very carefully. What it does mean is that, for example, when Mrs Tancred's in the room, Johnny's onstage in the bed; he's not behind the cretonne hanging, which is what O'Casey suggested, he's in a downstage corner. That means that one little section of the audience can look at Mrs Tancred, and Johnny's between them and her. It's almost like a cinematic shot, a close-up, which is terribly affecting and means you have an emotional pressure cooker in that space. You can very gently and very consistently keep turning up the pressure on it until it's explosive in Act Three. It's very carefully pitched; it's the easiest thing in the world to get people to shout, but to get it real, and then to let the explosions of emotion happen is what we were after.

You mentioned that Joe Dowling pointed up the contemporary resonances of the play; is that something you were conscious of doing?
They're there, but I don't draw them out. I try to get the specific world of the play right, and if you get the specifics right with O'Casey the universal aspects begin to be very apparent. I think it's dangerous to try and nudge an audience towards the contemporary resonance. That said, there is one costume that we left with an almost European feel to it, which is Mrs Tancred's costume. It's completely Irish, it's completely period, and yet if you took a photograph of it and told me it was a photograph of a Serbian woman, I'd believe you. That's more subliminal; it's not inviting the audience to make a link, just gently letting a connection be drawn. I don't believe in spelling things out for an audience. I hate being patronized myself when I go to the theatre, and so I feel quite strongly that you've got to present an audience with an open experience. They've got to do the work and piece it together. It's like pre-masticated food otherwise, and I can't see the point of that. It's better to be very clear with the story – lay out all the pieces on the floor in front of an audience and invite them to piece it together and draw their own connections.

The play is a great play because of the way it captures universal themes in an incredibly specific situation. My worry about us nudging an audience towards a contemporary political situation is that in some sense you diminish what he was actually writing about, which was the Irish Civil War. The themes he found in that are to do with abstract hatreds and with how some men will use language to avoid work, and others will use language to make people shoot each other. That's as relevant today, and in any political situation today, as it was then. He's right on the money there. But the designer and I also discussed how we were going to handle this play for a London audience in 1999 when, let's face it, ninety to ninety-eight per cent of them couldn't tell you enough background information about the Irish Civil War to get on with the play. They barely know about it. They may know that there was one, and certainly after the Neil Jordan film they know who Michael Collins was, but not the details. If we wanted to take an approach to the piece which was almost in the form of what we used to call, in shorthand, 'documentary realism', then perhaps it might be appropriate for us to create a framework around the play involving documentary footage of the period. We entertained the notion for a while that we could open with projections of what the streets looked like in the period. There are two archive films available on video cassette, very rough, black-and-white shots of the War of Independence and the Civil War and there are some extraordinary shots in there of republican funerals, and fighting on O'Connell Street. We debated long and hard whether that might be an interesting way into the piece in 1999: that an audience would look at four minutes of this material and then we would focus in on one figure in the crowd and start off Johnny's story. Eventually, though, we decided against that, because I felt that, while it might have made for quite an interesting theatrical opening, it would have burdened the play with a weight of history which potentially it might not have recovered from. If you're giving an audience a history lesson for five minutes, which is essentially what we would have been doing, the audience then starts to look at a play in very different terms.

O'Casey writes so well about politics, as opposed to politicians. He's so much more interested, in the Dublin Trilogy, in what happens to the common people on the street and how events of the political dance happening above them trickle down and effect them. It's much more interesting using that as a prism through which to view political events and I thought that, if we started burdening the play with footage of the real historical events, there was a risk of alienating the audience by reminding them of how little they knew. If instead you begin the play and point up the fact that it's in a tenement house in Dublin, that it opens with somebody reading an account of how somebody upstairs was shot, your immediate engagement is on the level of the story. You watch Johnny snapping at Mary in the first five minutes, and you're only following what *these* people know about that story. It made us place an enormous amount of emphasis on debating how every single character has an attitude to the events in the play and what those attitudes are. They need to be lucid and crystal clear with that at all stages, because if there is any ambiguity in the acting the audience would certainly be lost. They have to work really hard for an audience, to let them know what a Diehard is; is it a good thing or a bad thing? is it something that you speak slightly hushed about? or is it something you can speak out about? The audience then gets a sense, when Boyle's talking about the Diehards, that they were an illegal force; it's as though you're a member of the IRA, you wouldn't want to broadcast it. So removing ourselves from the documentary approach placed all the more emphasis on every line of the play. I think that in a space like this you can do that, because you can make every word matter, and can point up the gap between what a character says and what they mean. You can make it very clear, without telling an audience what they should think about it, and an audience will actually draw their own conclusions from it.

So this shifts the burden of having the historical knowledge from the audience to the actors?

Absolutely. It placed a lot of importance on that. Having robbed ourselves of the opportunity of giving the audience a history lesson for three minutes before, it then meant that we would have to be really sure-footed. I set the actors research topics before they started rehearsals and whatever they couldn't find books on, I'd help them out with. We found information on the tenements in Dublin, and on the political situation, of course. So for Johnny Boyle, I sent William Ash after Michael Collins and I said, 'Go after his education, find out about how he was educated and about this blacksmith character who taught him everything he knows about republicanism.' If you give an actor a doorway into the sort of questions to ask about a big historical character like Michael Collins, suddenly he has the means to find out how someone like Johnny would have become inculcated with republicanism, to the extent that by the age of sixteen he's a wounded war veteran. Those things then take on a greater degree of reality. We live in a world where we don't have contact with bullets and bombs, and if you're playing with characters who do, you have to do your homework properly. Consequently, we sent them off to doctors to find out what a bullet wound in the hip would do, what a bomb shattering an arm would look like, did careful homework. Renée Weldon, who played Mary, found out about the strikes in the period, and the Labour movement and how usual it was for a girl of that age to be reading Ibsen plays at the time. With Bentham, the question was what kind of creature does he want to be when he talks about the Prawna and theosophy; apart from him being the butt of jokes, what's beneath it? What about Captain Boyle talking about being a seafaring man, when everyone knows he was never on the sea except for once on a collier from Dublin to Liverpool – what kind of a man needs the world to believe that he was a great seafaring man? You get into the area of someone who's long term unemployed, whose self-esteem is probably through the ground, who's got no sense of being the breadwinner, and then a different kind of personality opens up which is probably a bit more vulnerable, a bit more fractious, and the drinking begins to make sense. It's not just that tautological nonsense that he drinks because he's Irish. You begin to examine the conditions that O'Casey was writing about and try and rethink it, and find a fresh way into it.

Then there's Joxer, a character who's a form of non-character. He's like a Rorschach test: you can see whatever you want to see when you look at him; he can reflect back at you whatever he thinks you want to hear. He's a yes-man, and to try and imbue that character with some sense of a pre-history that is maybe sad, rather than him just being a gag-meister, is the task. Why is this man living in a tenement quoting reams of nineteenth-century poetry and social commentary? He's got a phrase for every single situation, so where did that come from? From what we know biographically that's pretty close to O'Casey's heart. It's the kind of education that O'Casey gave himself, collecting all those books and memorizing chunks of them, but he's a deft writer, and he made this character who's a tissue of quotations from other people; he's almost a post-modern character! The task is to latch that on to reality, to root it, because you can see the truth in the actors' eyes in that space in a way you can't in a proscenium-arch space. Likewise, I sent the actor who was playing Jerry Devine to find out all about the Labour movement and James Connolly; I got the actor playing the Mobiliser to research Tom Barry's guerrilla days in Ireland, actual accounts of how far those men were willing to go, lying in wait in ambush sometimes for thirty-six hours without moving, without eating, in a damp ditch. The kind of extremism, the kind of leverage that you get from an extremely held political opinion, was the thing that we had to get right into those boys' heads. I don't think anybody of my generation really believes in dying for their country, so in order to play a character who does, you have to ask, what would you die for? So when Johnny says, 'No man can do enough for Ireland', what does that mean? Then, of course, there's the issue of

Johnny's disaffection with republicanism, and indeed how you make sense of him squealing on Tancred.

It almost feels as if Johnny's story is one draft short, and if you look at the first draft of the play, Johnny's story is far less significant. It's almost as if O'Casey realized he had struck on a very rich seam with Johnny's story. It was based on an anecdote from a girl who lived in the house in the North Circular Road, where he wrote the play, and it's almost as if, having written the first draft, he discovered the character of Johnny, and in the second draft wrote him up enormously. I think, though, that he still leaves us one piece of dramaturgical information short. It's possible to deduce that Johnny betrayed Tancred to the CID men bursting into the house, but why? We never know why, and the only reason I can put forward is his disaffection with republicanism, and the emptiness and hollowness of his 'I'd do it again, Ma, a principle's a principle,' or, 'Ireland only half free will never be at peace while she's a son left to pull a trigger'. We tried to suggest that, instead of those being passionately held convictions, they've the hollow ring of clichés, that in some sense Johnny ultimately has to cling on to a shell of republicanism because it's his trump card. He's a wounded war veteran and that keeps away the suspicion that he could possibly have anything to do with betraying a comrade. He has to play that role all the more but there's something shrill about it. One wants more information about Johnny for it to fully make sense.

And this all follows from shifting the focus away from Juno and the Captain?
I think it makes you realize what a rich dramatic canvas the man has created, because Mary's story also takes on an incredible poignancy in that sense. I think Jerry and Mary's second scene, where she tells him she's pregnant, is the most difficult scene in the play. To get the right pitch to his betrayal of her is a very tricky thing to do. I think that, as a character, Jerry Devine is probably closest to O'Casey's centre of gravity, in the

sense of his being a Labour leader, and in the sense of his world view; but then when Jerry rejects Mary, if you get it right, it's all the more shocking because he's supposed to be the 'good' character; it doesn't make sense. It's almost as if O'Casey's wandering into the territory of the end of *King Lear* and the death of Cordelia. You cross the line and it seems that all political convictions are fundamentally bogus and that he doesn't trust any man's ability to be consistent with his words, and winds up celebrating the resilience of a woman who can be knocked down repeatedly and yet stand up, bless herself and go on. I think he actually has a grudging respect for the strength that Juno's faith gives her, not for the faith itself but in that as a function of that woman's make-up.

Once you approach it in this way the other aspect that comes out more strongly is the family. We've gone after it as a family unit. What comes through from his writing is that those two kids, Johnny and Mary, represent aspects of Juno and the Captain. If you draw that out, Mary has got all of the Captain's self-righteous snottiness and hates being challenged. When the play opens, she knows about the will, but she hasn't said anything to her mother, and in Act Three that's mirrored with the Captain knowing that the will is a washout and not saying anything to Juno. And Johnny and Juno I think have almost a closer relationship, if anything, than Juno and Mary, because Juno and Mary are often bickering, whereas Juno indulges Johnny a lot more. Johnny snaps at them, 'Oh, quit that readin', for God's sake! Are yous losin' all your feelin's? It'll soon be that none of you'll read anythin' that's not about butcherin'!' and storms out of the room, to which Mary replies, 'He's gettin' very sensitive all of a sudden!' within earshot of him, which is a classic image of a brother and sister starting a row; and then Juno steps in and says, 'I'll read it myself, Mary, by an' by, when I come home.' She'll never come down against Johnny. She says to him, 'go back and lie down again, and I'll bring you in a nice cup o' tay,' and Johnny says, 'Tay, tay, tay! You're always thinkin' o' tay. If a man was dyin' you'd thry to make him swally a cup o' tay,' and the door slams again. She never tackles him, whereas with the Captain, she'll be straight in and she'll take him on and she'll take Mary on: 'I don't know what a girl on strike wants to be wearin' a ribbon round her head for, or silk stockins on her legs either.' But Johnny is the darling, and it's brilliantly observed in that way. It's also interesting that the Captain has no relationship with Johnny in the play to speak of, none, and in a way they both have a particular illusion about themselves that they present to the world; for one it's based on Republicanism, and for the other it's an illusion based on his seafaring days.

We tried to stitch in a number of moments where the Captain is very aware of Johnny. For example, after the knocking at the door in Act One, the Captain comes back in and he says, 'It's a fella in a trench coat,' and Johnny starts praying, 'Holy Mary, Mother o' God,' and the Captain says, 'He's goin' away.' We've just drawn out the moment of the Captain watching Johnny, not quite knowing why his own son is reacting in insane terror at somebody knocking on the door. Similarly, in Act Two, we've stitched in a moment where, just before the gramophone arrives, Johnny enters the room, and Boyle looks as if he's about to say something to him. O'Casey suggests that, and so again, we've given it an emphasis. It's a case of trying to get those moments where a character is aware of another character but not quite sure of what's going on in their life. That notion is central again with Juno, because you can ask, is Juno stupid that she doesn't see these things going on? Does she not suspect that Johnny's involved with Tancred? And in some sense, I don't think she does suspect that Johnny is involved with Tancred, and to pull that off without her looking stupid, you've got to stitch in a degree of deliberately not wanting to see that her own son is involved in anything bad. Now that he's a wounded war veteran, she needs to cling on to the notion that he's out of the game, that he has nothing to do with it. So when she says, 'Thanks be to God that Johnny had nothin' to do with him this long time,' at the start of the play when everybody's saying he's a Diehard, we had to make it very clear that this is somebody who's convincing herself. Even though she is saying, 'Thank God he has nothing to do with it,' there's a nervousness in the back of her head: once you're a member of an organization like that do you ever really leave?

Do you have plans for other productions of O'Casey's work?
I'd love to do more O'Casey; *The Plough and the Stars*, maybe and I'd love to do *Cock-a-Doodle Dandy*. The madness of it appeals to me, and I don't quite know why, because I've never seen a performance of it. I'm curious about how to make that piece work – it's an intriguing play – but not for a while. I'll let this run its course and go away and do other work, even though I'm in love with his world and his writing. Very often that's not the best time to go on to a second project. It's probably best to go on and do other things and then come back to it, but I will definitely do more O'Casey. The fabric of the writing is just the finest that I've worked with. I adore working on Shakespeare as well, but it doesn't quite reach the parts that O'Casey reaches. I don't know whether that's being Irish or not, but it's just an absolute privilege to work on a play like this – genuinely, there's not many plays I'd say that about. It wasn't like work at all: it was the happiest time I've ever had in rehearsal, but then we had a fantastic cast and they worked brilliantly together.

Dearbhla Molloy
Dearbhla Molloy, who began her career as an actor at the Abbey Theatre in Dublin, took the role of Juno in John Crowley's production.

Was the approach taken in the Donmar Warehouse production of Juno and the Paycock *very different from that of the other productions in which you've been involved?*
Trevor Nunn used a similar approach, in his production with Judi Dench playing Juno. He gave everybody themes that they had to explore. Mine, as Mary, was the state of women in

trades unions in Ireland; Judi's was Irish tenement life at the time; John Rogan, who played Joxer, looked at popular entertainment of the day; and Johnny researched the background to the Civil War. Then we had a whole day where everybody had to read the papers they'd written, so that we were all singing from the same hymn sheet, so to speak, when it actually came to doing the production. That's also the approach that we used in this production, because it pays such enormous dividends.

There are particular problems with *Juno*. When I first started at the Abbey, there were people there who'd been in the original production, and there were generalized, unchallenged assumptions about the piece that then automatically came into play when it was staged. So Juno was a certain shape, Joxer was a certain size, the Captain was always played in a certain way, and when we actually did all the research, a lot of these assumptions proved to be false. For example, it was always generally assumed in Irish productions that Johnny's arm had been blown off in the fighting in O'Connell Street in 1916, but we discovered that there was fighting in O'Connell Street only a few months before the start of the action. Now that makes an enormous difference to the dynamic of the family, because this is a family that's obviously lived reasonably well until Johnny and Mary are both taken out as wage earners. The Captain has been able to coast, because he's been living off the other three, but suddenly there are four adults with only one of them earning, and that's Juno. The only two jobs that she could have had, given the fact that she's allowed to go in her own time and isn't afraid of being fired, were to be a scrubber or what was called a 'tugger'. Those were people who pushed carts round the outskirts of the city to the more affluent suburbs and got cast-off clothes, brought them back, cleaned them up, did a bit of patching and then sold them on the markets. Well, if I'd chosen to be that character, to do that job, I couldn't have made it visible to the audience. So I made her a scrubber, so that I could show the tools of the trade, which were the scrubbing brush, the bucket and the second apron.

In some ways this production wasn't terribly different from Trevor's, apart from the fact that it wasn't in a proscenium-arch theatre. It wasn't different in its ethos, but there were other differences, because it's twenty years later and you always bring the sensibility of the time to bear on whatever classic you're doing, consciously or unconsciously. I know that the attitudes of the two younger people who played Mary and Johnny were very different from my attitudes way back when I played Mary, because they're children of the nineties and I was a child of the sixties. That was very interesting, and also, because we're playing it on a three-sided stage and because the audience are so close, and aren't separated by either an orchestra pit, or the height that a proscenium stage is usually at, it means that the audience feel that they are in the room with us. I think that both that feeling of being in the room and the fact that we played to three sides also affects the comedy. I don't know whether that's a good thing or a bad thing, but it definitely has an effect. If we ever did it again, I would like to do that scale of production in a proscenium-arch theatre. Then, hopefully, you could get the intimacy that we had in this production, but you would also be able to focus on the comedy. What happens on a three-sided stage is that there are always two lots of people who don't get it, because they can't see your face.

Trevor's production was such a landmark production that quite a lot of things I learned from it are still with me, but the greatest obstacle, really, to my playing Juno, was the fact that Judi Dench had played her. She's such an icon, and she is the actor I most admire; she's the only actor that I could really attach the word 'great' to. So to follow that was quite scary. My fear was that I would be unconsciously copying her, and would never make the role mine, so for a while I did things deliberately in antithesis to how she had done them, which didn't necessarily serve the play. For example the final scene: it took me a long time to get that because I didn't want to do it the way she did it, so I had to break through that. That was the biggest thing really. The rest of the action is based on the relationship which you evolve with the person who's playing your husband or your child or your neighbour, and I gradually shed that fear of being like her, but the last speech is such a big thing in the Irish canon, that I wanted to find my own way through it and I found it really difficult to get her voice out of my head.

Would you agree that, compared with, say, Nora in The Plough and the Stars, *Mary and Juno are O'Casey's strongest roles for women?*

Nora hasn't developed into a strong woman yet. Maybe the tragedy that she goes through is what allows her to become a Juno eventually. Mary you can play in a lot of different ways. When I played Mary, I always assumed that she was going to become Juno at some point. I don't know whether Renée Weldon, who played her this time, had the same notion, but she certainly played it quite differently. I purposely modelled myself on my mother, if you like. I don't think Renée necessarily did that. I've never had the desire to play Nora and I never have played her, because I've always thought she was quite wet, to be honest. It may be that a young female actor looking at it now would see possibilities, in the light of contemporary sensibilities, which I didn't see when I was at the right age to play her. There's no doubt that O'Casey's women are stronger than the men, not as characters to play, but as human beings. I think his regard for men is pretty low, especially if you look at *Juno* and the parts men play in it. What I wanted to do in this production was to show the life they could have had, had their financial circumstances been different. In many productions that I've seen there's been no sense of a relationship between the Captain and Juno, and I've never believed that. I've always wanted to see why they got together and I want to see what they would have been like when they were good together. That's why we introduced, as much as possible, echoes of their early relationship, which you should be able to see in the party scene. I think that then makes it all the more horrible and all the more tragic in the end; but you should also be able to see

that there's a co-dependency going on here, that Juno has facilitated her own tragedy. What Johnny says is true: 'You're to
blame yourself for a gradle of it – givin' him his own way in
everything . . . why didn't you look afther th' money?' And
that's true, Juno has facilitated his alcoholism for one thing,
and O'Casey displays that beautifully when she has that enormous row with him at the beginning of the third act. She asks
him why he doesn't get up and go and see about the money
because they're in terrible debt – to owe £20 to Annie Murphy
is the equivalent to a huge amount now – and then he says to
her, 'Is there a bottle of stout left?' and she says, 'There's two of
them here,' and she passes one in to him. So she absolutely
facilitates their tragedy and I wanted to make that clear. I do
think truly that she is a martyr, because she keeps saying, 'I'll
face th'ordeal meself,' or, 'your poor oul' selfish mother was
only thinkin' of herself,' all those kinds of things that can actually be quite irritating, but I decided to play against that as
much as I could. I was concerned that the audience wouldn't be
able to empathize with her. I don't know whether that's right or
wrong, but that was my choice. And it may be that one of the
reasons for the choice I made is that kind of woman with both
those sides to her character, the martyr and the saint, was very
recognizable in Irish culture, but I haven't really seen her in
English culture. I was afraid that she wouldn't be recognized
and wouldn't be forgiven by an English audience if I empha-
sized those aspects.

Joxer and the Captain are only afraid of her because they
want an easy life. She gives them grief, but they're not physically afraid of her. It's just that they'd have to explain themselves, which they can't do because they've got no justification
for how they are. We don't know what Joxer's life is like, but it
seems that his involvement with women is minimal, so he's
probably terrified of them. It has to be plain that being faced by
a harridan like Juno must be quite scary for a man who lives
this ghastly bachelor existence, whose only friend is his pint.
When they try to get him to sing at the party, there's a sense

that he would be far more at ease doing that in the snug, because the snug was a male preserve. He'd probably be fine in that cosy, alcohol suffused environment, but he's not so happy sitting there with a hostess who doesn't like him.

The key question for me, though, was why Juno leaves when she does, because it was such a huge thing then. My research threw up the fact that you made your bed and you lay on it; you married and it was for life. For her to say she'd leave and never come back again, and let him fend for himself, would have been an enormous thing. The second thing was that she stood by Mary, and that was a huge step to take. In those times girls who became pregnant were normally thrown out by their families. Johnny's attitude would be perfectly normal, as would the father's. Women in that situation would become prostitutes and they would die pretty soon. I had to figure out why Juno would react the way she does. Of course in those days people had no contraception and had huge families, so I wondered why Juno and Jack have only got two children, what happened to the other pregnancies? It must have been either that she and the Captain never slept together, which means a whole different kind of relationship, which was not the relationship I wanted to go for, or that they had had children or pregnancies and that the children had died. The only clue is Maisie Madigan saying, '. . . an' I remember sayin' to Joxer, there, who I met comin' up th' stairs, that the new arrival in Boyle's ud grow up a hardy chiselur if it lived,' and it's the 'if it lived' that's the key, because most of them didn't.

So I thought that she'd transferred her passion on to the children, for good and bad reasons. The negative would be that she's a very controlling woman and so she could control them in a way she couldn't really control Jack. But then Jack controls things by his alcoholism; he dictates the economics of the family. So I wanted to make it a very physical relationship with those two children and I wanted the audience to be quite clear that she was passionate about them so that when Johnny is dead a constellation of emotional and psychological factors come into play. When Johnny dies, Mary's response needed to be enormous, to the extent that Juno, in the way I chose to play her, is afraid that she'll tumble into complete nihilism. Faith's the only thing that kept those people going, and I wanted to give Juno a very powerful faith. That's what has kept her going, and she knows, on some level, that if Mary is to survive, she's going to have to have faith, and if Mary says, 'There isn't a God,' Mary's dead, in Juno's view. So she has to inject faith back into her. The first thing she says is, 'These things have nothin' to do with the Will o' God. Ah, what can God do agen the stupidity o' men?' The only way she can be sure that Mary will survive is to look after her, and that's the good reason for doing it. The negative reasons are that she'll have another thing that she can control, and have power over, the child, and she can have a primary function in a life again, which she wouldn't have if Mary went off and if she was left with Jack. She makes an instant decision to go, and this was the only way that I could make emotional logic of her journey. I worked back from the relationship with the children, and I hoped the audience would follow that logic too.

I don't know what will happen with her and Jack. The fact is that she will have to come back, she'll have to get her belongings and clear the place out, and they have to meet at Johnny's funeral. There are all sorts of possibilities. I've no doubt that she'll go and live with Mary at her sister's until the baby's born and then I've no doubt that she and Mary will live together, but whether Jack's part of it I don't know. I think there's a possibility that Jack may not survive the night because it's very cold, it's November, there's no heat, he's lying on the floor. He may well die and I think that's implicit in him being left. Or will he become like Joxer, living off other people? The future's bleak, to say the least of it, and that's got to be part of the tragedy too.

How important do you think it is to fill in the wider historical context of the play?

I think that from an audience point of view it doesn't really matter so much because they get enough information from the play itself. The only thing they need to cotton on to that maybe we should have made a bit more of, is the fact that Johnny's illness is recent. O'Casey himself doesn't make it clear; the only reference is when Juno says, 'The bullet he got in the hip in Easter Week was bad enough, but the bomb that shatthered his arm in the fight in O'Connell Street put the finishin' touch on him . . . I went down on my bended knees to him not to go agen the Free State.' Well the Free State was only just declared, which is the clue to fact that he was damaged going against the Free State. It's pretty obscure and it's the only thing that I think nowadays you'd have to take care of. I don't really think we could find a way to be graphic about that, but hopefully you got a sense that Johnny hasn't been an invalid for years and years. It's very difficult to do.

From the actor's point of view, I think you absolutely have to know the political context of the play, in this play much more so than in *The Plough and the Stars*. *Plough* is 1916 and there's a lot of available information, and a lot of common knowledge about the period, but I think the Civil War's much more subtle and much more complex to get a hold on. You need to be clear about what Diehards are and what republicans are, which side they were on, what the political affiliations of the house are. Some mother's son in the house betrays some other mother's son, who in turn betrays another mother's son and what's left are the mothers. This is another part of what O'Casey's saying and it comes through in that wonderful speech that Mrs Tancred has: 'An' now here's the two of us oul' women, standin' one on each side of a scales o' sorra, balanced be the bodies of our two dead darlin' sons.' Every night those words always had such a profound effect on me. We performed this play in the aftermath of Kosovo, in the aftermath of Bosnia, and at the time East Timor was going on and I just thought, *There are mothers all over the world with sons on either side, and what's the point of it all?* I think it was very important for us as actors to be very clear about what the political context of the play was, but it's not so hugely important for the audience. So long as they know it's a Civil War, it doesn't matter if they don't know exactly what a Diehard was or what a Republican was, so long as they know they were each on opposite sides

He's a wonderful writer. Another thing that we weren't able to explore in this production, because it was a chamber production, is the sensuality of the language. On a proscenium stage, because you can be slightly bigger, you can then explore that language in your mouth much more than you can when the audience is so close to you. Wonderful phrases, wonderful stitching together of words, like jewels.

Andy Arnold

Andy Arnold is artistic director of The Arches, Glasgow, where he has directed productions of *Purple Dust* (1994) and *Cock-a-Doodle Dandy* (1996).

The Arches is an arts centre. We've got a hundred-seat studio theatre and also a larger hundred-and-sixty-seat space. They're in Victorian, brick-built, arched spaces underneath Glasgow Central railway station that are very atmospheric, decaying and crumbling, particularly the studio theatre, so I tend to choose plays which fit into that environment. *Purple Dust* was originally designed for here, and then we took it on to the Tron Theatre, and *Cock-a-Doodle Dandy* was a joint production that we performed at the Tron in 1996. I knew of O'Casey's major works, which I very much enjoy, but I didn't know his later works at all. Then my wife, Muireann Kelly, who's an Irish actress, and who performed in the Abbey production of *Purple Dust* many years ago, said she thought *Purple Dust* would be a great play to do at the Arches and that it would fit in well with our style of theatre. We have a wide repertoire. Sometimes we do haunting, performance art-type pieces, so for example we once did an adaptation of the film *Metropolis*; but we've done Pinter plays and we also had a reputation, particularly in the early nineties, for doing highly irreverent comedies. There are a lot of Irish plays that fall into that category and that's been our house style, if you like. The first one of those we did was Brendan Behan's *Richard's Cork Leg*, which was very successful. I tend to work with an ensemble of actors who have an anarchic performance style and who also play musical instruments. When I came across *Purple Dust*, here was a play with songs in it, which is completely mad and which seemed to fit in very well with the Arches style of theatre. I thought it would be great fun to do and because it is set in a crumbling old mansion, we could design it very easily for this space.

In the studio, we've got movable banks of seating that can be put in any configuration, so we're not restricted to being in the round. We're spending £4 million on building refurbishment next year. We want to keep the atmosphere, but get rid of the damp! It'll be very exciting, but we want to hold on to the rawness. It's a terrific theatre space, so it lends itself to a type of rough theatre that is very much in the spirit of those later O'Casey plays. *Cock-a-Doodle Dandy* is a completely surreal piece but *Purple Dust*, although again it's a farce, is a bit more contained in reality. In some respects they're very similar: the central characters in both plays are buffoons, two old Irishmen in *Cock-a-Doodle Dandy* and two English buffoons in the other. I played Basil Stokes in *Purple Dust* and I played Old Shanaar, the old man at the end of *Cock-a-Doodle Dandy*. Both plays also have wild young women and rebellious maids – Maria in one and Cloyne in the other – and rebellious workmen, the local navvies who are that bit sharper than the other characters. I think the message in one is slightly different from the message in the other, though; *Purple Dust* is really a lighthearted stab at English imperialism, pointing up the richness of poetry as opposed to the material wealth of the two English men, whereas *Cock-a-Doodle Dandy* is more a stab at the old traditions of Ireland itself; there are no outsiders involved at all. It tackles patriarchal views, particularly those of the

Catholic Church, which was why it was banned in Ireland for so long.

I think farce dominates in *Purple Dust*. It's a hilarious play, but it's also a very long play. We cut it quite a bit, actually. I think a lot of the points are repeated through the workmen's speeches; they're eloquent but they do start to repeat themselves after a while. I wouldn't say that it's really making a political point. In some respects it's taking a situation which is a very common one, then treating it in a totally ridiculous way. There is passion in it; the serious characters are the Irish labourers really; they're the ones who express O'Casey's argument, that the English can't understand the values system of the Irish. Both plays are obviously a rather romantic view of Ireland from across the water, but *Cock-a-Doodle Dandy* definitely has a nasty edge to it, particularly towards the end. The whole thing becomes very serious, although even then it's tinged with ridiculously black humour. At the very end of the play Lorna's sister is brought back from Lourdes and that whole journey has been a failure. We had the sister going off, but we didn't have her coming back, because we felt that suddenly bringing that character back would have undermined the climax of the play. So there is a serious edge to it and it's very important that that's there. I think you undersell the play if you just go for laughs, although serious points can be got across through humour. Father Domineer is a hilarious character, and Grant Sweeney, the actor who played him in our production, was hysterically funny; everybody on stage was shaking with laughter sometimes. But if you just went for the humour the piece wouldn't work. If you just made it a rollicking farce, it wouldn't have a point. You have to get across what O'Casey was trying to get across, but whereas the Dublin plays are steeped in reality and real-life situations, these are a fairly cynical view of a country where he's no longer living.

James Joyce never wrote about the rural situation – he regarded Ireland almost as a joke when he left – but O'Casey decided to take it on, and was criticized for that decision. It's all right to be an ambassador for your country when you live abroad, but if you have a snipe, particularly at the Catholic Church, it goes against you. *Purple Dust*, on the other hand, was sniping at the English; but they're very clever farces, just from the point of view of the actual business. It was a lot of fun just trying to work out how to do *Cock-a-Doodle Dandy*. When I read the script I thought it was a very confused piece of writing, but as a director, I got very caught up in the visual images: things getting thrown out of the windows, this cock bird charging round the place, the top hat getting shot off, and the bottle of whiskey suddenly glowing red hot. Just the mechanics of it is all good fun. In *Purple Dust*, as well, you've got scenes that worked brilliantly in here – when they move the furniture in, for instance: it was meant to be a very expensive sideboard that they're bringing in, and they're bashing it about, but because there was a lot of music in the play, we decided to drag in a piano, and it just got completely wrecked as it was pulled in. Then, at the end of the play, when the flood took place, the piano started playing by itself, which was good fun. They're very busy farces and I think that, of their time, and for somebody of the age he was then, they're very surreal and very contemporary in their style. It's almost a *commedia dell'arte* style, and at times it was like doing a Dario Fo farce: complete mayhem, but very well-structured.

The actors loved doing it and it was perfect for the Arches Company to be doing, and perfect for the space. We took it to the Tron and it was good there, but for me it didn't have the same atmosphere. We have the old archways and, in terms of building the set, all we had to do was put a load of scaffolding and scaffold boards, and some old bits of plaster work and cornices, up on the back wall and then drape some old dustsheets around, and that was it. With a few bits of old furniture it looked like a grand room. The Tron, on the other hand, is an end-on space, a black-box type auditorium in a converted church. It's a much bigger space than we have here, and making it feel like an ancestral room was harder. One nice thing, though, was that high up on the back wall they have stained-glass windows, which are boarded over, and at the end, when we climbed up in the flood, we uncovered the windows and it gave just an extra little visual element. *Purple Dust* can seem quite a cumbersome piece, but by being fairly liberal with it and doing it in a style which I think O'Casey would have approved of, and belting out the songs, we made it work. I was very nervous about it beforehand, and at the first read-through of the script there weren't that many laughs; the whole thing seemed rather overwritten. But once we started to work on it and make the thing come alive, we just loved it.

Do you have a fixed company here?
We have visiting companies here, but we do four Arches Theatre Company productions a year, so we don't have a continual repertory situation, but during that period some of these actors were in several shows. Half of the cast in *Purple Dust* were from Ireland and in Glasgow you get an awful lot of second-generation Irish, so there's no problem with the accents. The only person who's appalling at accents is me, but it's such an irreverent piece that it didn't really matter. I think I got fussier over the years, actually. With *Richard's Cork Leg* it didn't really matter because it was such a chaotic production, whereas we did Sebastian Barry's *Boss Grady's Boys* a couple of years ago, a wonderful poetic play about two old brothers living in the West of Ireland, and I auditioned old Irish actors in Dublin. The play is set on the Cork–Kerry border, and it was absolutely crucial, as far as I was concerned, to get the rhythms of speech. Those accents were totally genuine, whereas you can take more liberty with these less realistic plays.

Did you feel that Purple Dust *had particular resonance for a Scottish audience?*
O'Casey must have been very aware of the English attitude towards the Irish, the lack of understanding and the failure to give any positive value to Irish heritage or intellect, particularly

in the south of England; but there's also the fact that, historically, the Irish are so much more sophisticated in their development of language and literature. To me the most evocative portrayal of that is Brian Friel's play *Translations*, which expresses those sentiments beautifully, without anybody actually making any explicit political statement. I can't stand the more didactic agitprop theatre that just tells you what the situation is and what you should think about it. Friel's play just shows the characters and the situation, and it speaks volumes. The Scots, though, don't have that same literary tradition. They have the Celtic language, but they don't have the same tradition of literature or poetry, certainly not plays. I don't know why that is; it's a marvel, really, the number of world-class playwrights still coming out of that Ireland, whereas in Scotland there are very few; it's a different type of tradition. Nonetheless, I think the whole attitude of the English to the Scots is very similar, so in Glasgow those very eloquent speeches lambasting the English certainly hit a chord. I don't know why the play hasn't been revived more often. I thought ours was, in fact, the first Scottish production, but there was an amateur production in the forties.

So we did *Purple Dust* in January 1994 and then again in June at the Tron, and in 1996 we did a co-production with the Tron of *Cock-a-Doodle Dandy*. We built a set, all in vac-form polystyrene, so it was a complete facade of the front of the house, totally naturalistic in appearance, and all the action took place in the garden. The audience thought they were looking at a naturalistic piece and then this huge bird comes running on stage. One of the actors played several of the smaller parts and so he would go off and then come on as the cock bird. It was a full costume, wonderfully made, and it worked brilliantly. You saw silhouettes of it through the window early on, but you didn't really expect to actually see the bird. At the end of the first act, though, when they're just sitting there quietly in the garden in the darkness and start singing a song, the bird came on and started dancing away.

But the politics of the piece are strange. The women are the serious characters, but it's very difficult to know what the message of it is supposed to be. Is it politically correct that we're doing this now, or is it just a misogynist bit of nonsense? But then the women do come out top in the end. The absurd characters are the old men, who are very hypocritical: one of them is berating his daughter at the same time as chatting up the maid and the other one, Mahon, chats up Loreleen. There's something fairly nasty about both of them and because of that I think your sympathies are definitely with the women. They are all a bit one-dimensional, though, and there's no intellectual argument that comes out through the women, not like you get with the workmen in *Purple Dust*. Here it's much more a case of expressing particular emotions, deriding the old characters, but not really presenting an argument.

Everyone enjoyed *Cock-a-Doodle Dandy* – it was great fun – but they came away a bit confused about what the message was supposed to be, particularly at the end when it gets very serious. It can seem as though the ending has been tagged on; there's a lot of reactionary bile all the way through and at the end they get their come-uppance, but it doesn't really come from anywhere. It's not such a well-constructed piece, really, but the language is so lovely and rich, and that's why I like doing O'Casey's plays. It's highly romanticized in a way, very lyrical, but the actors really enjoy it, although it's very difficult, particularly for non-Irish actors to actually deliver some of the lines, which are quite convoluted – incredibly so in this later work.

A lot of our shows are for a young audience. We run a nightclub here as well, which funds the theatre side. When we do plays like O'Casey, we do bring in an older audience, but we aim to bring in young people and people who don't normally go to the theatre. It's not always achievable, but it's great when you can do it.

Shivaun O'Casey

Shivaun O'Casey was born in 1939 in Devon. She studied scenic design at the Central School of Arts and Crafts, and acting at RADA and the Drama Centre, London. She toured America twice, first with the Dublin Players and later with Theatre 61. She assisted Alan Schneider before joining the Bristol Old Vic as assistant scenic designer. Here she worked with directors Frank Dunlop, John Neville, Robin Phillips and Peter Duguid. As an actress she worked in repertory companies, the West End, television and film with Stephen Frears, Peter Gill, Jack MacGowran, Anthony Hopkins, Ian McKellen and others. When she became a mother she gave up theatre for some years, turning instead to teaching, and running an art gallery. In 1987 she started directing and producing with Samuel Beckett's *Happy Days* followed by Frank McGuinness's *Baglady* and her father's play *Purple Dust*. In 1991 she formed the O'Casey Theater Company, based in both Northern Ireland and New York. The company's productions were used as a training base for local people, and Equity membership was obtained for several of the young trainees. The company produced three shows that toured internationally: *Shadow of a Gunman*, *Three Shouts from a Hill*, and *The Plough and the Stars* – and, for performance in Derry only, *Behind the Green Curtains*. Her most recent production was *Song at Sunset*, with Niall Buggy, a one-man show about her father that she compiled and directed. At present she is working on a documentary about her father with Albert Maysles and Mary Beth Yarrow.

From the interviews that Sean gave, it seems as though he felt that writers such as Harold Pinter and Samuel Beckett were rather pessimistic, and that he couldn't really see the point of writing those kinds of plays.

Sean was always very positive about the future and life, about the good in people; I mean he was very definite about the evil there was, and that came out more in his abstract plays, like in *Cock-a-Doodle Dandy*, where Father Domineer is such an evil character. In his earlier work, there's no one really evil; he loves them all, however awful they are, however sly: he sympathizes with Joxer, for example. *Cock-a-Doodle Dandy*'s full of humour, but it seems to have these very dramatic cruel moments that pull you up short; and I think the message is that it's in your hands, that you've got to fight for what you believe – at least, that's what I get out of it. He didn't like cruelty for the sake of being cruel, though, in the same way that he couldn't bear horror. I think that when he went to America first, in the thirties this would have been, he noticed many of the films were about death and violence, and he couldn't understand it. He'd say, 'What is this love of death, this necrolatry?' He writes about this in the last article he wrote, 'The Bald Primaqueera'.

Which of your father's plays have you directed?
I haven't really directed that much because I came to it so late in life. The first play of his I directed was *Purple Dust* at the Peacock Theatre, which I'm very proud of, actually. It was pulled to bits by the Dublin critics; they didn't really like the play, but at the previews the audiences loved it. The design was beautiful, really lovely; a young designer called Jan B. Brown designed the set and the costumes and they were colourful and witty. We did it on a shoestring, and we got a wonderful artist called Graham Nuttall, who worked a lot in papier mâché, to do the armour. He also made some flying ducks that flew out when the gun went off, and the cow's head, so none of it was 'realistic'. I really enjoyed working on that; I found it interesting, because there was music involved and song and a bit of dancing, many costumes. I think I did it the right way. I think it should be heightened in style, as Sean wanted.

After *Purple Dust* I directed *A Pound on Demand* in a theatre café on 42nd Street in New York. I had a gifted cast, with Colm Meany and Dennis Christopher playing the two drunks. After that I didn't direct anything of Sean's until I formed a theatre company in Northern Ireland. I was asked to form this company by the singer Tommy Sands. Its home was to be Newry, in Northern Ireland. We started with Sean's early work; we did *The Shadow of a Gunman*. I wanted to do his later work, but I thought it would be sensible for the young people involved to see his early work first and then later to see how he developed. I also wanted to do work that he admired or that had influenced him, such as George Bernard Shaw's *John Bull's Other Island*, and then it would be lovely to do some new work too. The first production in 1991 did very well. We built all the sets and we had apprentices attached to every aspect of the production, working and helping to build the sets, to paint the sets, to make the props and so on. Then we used local people wherever we could and on the first night you couldn't get in; it was great. Then we toured America. We were one of the first companies who forged an agreement with the three Equities: American, British and Irish. We had to agree to have one-third American Equity members, so we had one-third American, one-third British and one-third Irish. (Of course, British includes Northern Irish.) We managed to do that and they let us use American ASMs, and they're brilliant, so that was an advantage: to have wonderful stage management.

How did it work, having that mix of nationalities and accents?
I don't think accents matter too much – I mean, you might as well say you have to have Dubliners in the Dublin plays, the accents are so different all over Ireland. When you go to the Abbey and see *Shadow of a Gunman* or *Juno and the Paycock*, or *The Plough and the Stars*, they're often not all speaking with Dublin accents. Now there is something you can do: you can work on accents, and have a dialect coach come in and teach you. It's something that's been done in film for years, and it happens now in theatre – it's an accepted thing. The young girl who played Nora in our production of *Plough*, Madeleine Potter, was American and I was asked, 'Where did you find this amazing Dublin actress?' She worked at it; she worked extremely hard. You have to work hard to achieve results like

that. You can't go out to the pub every night. You have to take it seriously.

The O'Casey Theater Company lasted for six years; but the play I was really interested in doing was the last play of Sean's we did, *Behind the Green Curtains*, which hadn't been done before in the English-speaking world, except in a matinee series in New York. We didn't have long enough to rehearse and we couldn't tour it – we didn't have enough money. I decided, 'Let's mount it and not tour it and that's that.' The play had a cast of eighteen – a large cast. We also had a summer course attached to this production, with local students, and students from Leeds University. The students sat in on production meetings and rehearsals and worked with the artists attached to the production, and with the voice and movement coaches. They had sessions with a mask maker and took writing seminars, as well as doing scene studies.

So the summer school was an extension of the theatre company?
Yes, which was my idea, taken from the Old Vic Theatre School in London, run by Michel Saint-Denis, where all the students learned everything: the business side, how to run a theatre, how to make sets and costumes; and they could also watch the Old Vic Company in rehearsals and performance. They learned by watching, by osmosis, which I think is incredibly important. I think all theatre schools should be attached to a living theatre. The National should have a theatre school; the RSC should have a school attached to it; it's a terrible waste not to. At the Old Vic they were in the same building and you learned so much from working with, say, the set designers, and I knew this from having done it myself, from being an apprentice at the Bristol Old Vic.

How did you approach directing Behind the Green Curtains?
Well, by reading it and everything around it – knowing that it was a strange piece, the last piece he wrote, and that it didn't fit into any category; finding out its main objective: a battle against hypocrisy and fear. When Lennox Robinson died, because he

was Protestant, the Catholics weren't meant to attend his funeral; the message came from high up that if any Catholic did attend, they'd be excommunicated. So, in the first scene they're all wondering whether to go to this funeral, they're all going backwards and forwards. After this the play takes place in the rooms of a businessman, who just doesn't really have the courage of his convictions. He tries, but he doesn't have the guts to go against the status quo, or the powers that be. It's about hypocrisy, the hypocrisy you find particularly in a suppressed society like Ireland. Of course, in the end the young women and men go off to find a new life; it's positive although it's sad. It's an interesting piece to do, but it's a very difficult piece, because there's a lot of talk, a lot of dialogue and not a lot of action during a great part of it. We got a long way with it, I think, and it was a lovely group of people to work with.

Did you run workshops yourself?
I did a few, but I was directing, so that was my main occupation. The students sat in on rehearsals. They were in on the first production meeting where I talked with the designer, Pamela Howard, about the set, the costumes, and the concept of the production. I admire abstract theatre and experimental theatre, but I do like it to be based on excellence of craft and technique. I like watching people doing it who know how to perform, who've learnt their trade, who've learnt their craft, and I think it's a shame when you see young people not learning how to use their bodies, their voices and so on. OK, one's got imagination – hopefully one's got that – but I think it's better if this imagination grows and expresses itself from a solid base; that's my belief. Sometimes you see performers wallowing away in their own egomania and I think it's awful. And then you see a true artist, and you realize the amount of work that has gone into getting to a state to free the body and imagination. It's like being a sculptor: you've got to learn to use your tools and learn to use the material you work with – that's how I see it. I don't really think acting's any different.

Did you find it was necessary to explain the context of the play to the actors?

To the actors, yes, definitely, and to everyone involved in the production. For *Behind the Green Curtains* we did a lot of work on the period that he was talking about, the Church at the time, and the marches. In particular, we read articles and letters that he wrote at the time to give the actors a feel for it, and to be aware of the people that he had based the characters on; but we didn't have time to do enough work on physicality and style. For example, when you see a company like the Moscow Arts do a similar play – say *Dead Souls* – they exaggerate their characters. One day you'll see an actor being the young lead and another day you'll see him as a shrivelled old man, and you can't believe it's the same person because the physical change has been so great – but it's utterly believable, and it's utterly believable because of all the work that has gone on so that their emotions and their feelings and their thoughts are actual. Although they're exaggerated, they come from something real; they're not put on. To bring it to that standard takes time and hard work – well, time that we didn't have, so we didn't achieve that standard by any means; but it was a very good try and I think that most of the actors learnt a lot from it. I know I did.

Do you think that the scale and demands of these plays are the reasons they haven't been done?

One reason, yes; I don't think people know quite how to do them. I think the production of *Within the Gates* in New York in the early thirties understood the work – you can tell from looking at the photographs of the sets and costumes and the artists like Lilian Gish. In the same way, *The Silver Tassie*, when it was produced by Charles B. Cochran in 1929 with an Augustus John set, enhanced the greatness of the play. I mean maybe neither of those was an absolutely perfect production, but they were both *very* good. These plays can be expensive to produce, as they have large casts, but they are both a challenge and a reward. *The Silver Tassie* and *The Plough and the Stars* are both large works – what I call epic drama. I don't think *The Plough* is 'realistic' in the accepted sense of that word. That first scene in *The Plough* – the way it's written, you get this feeling of an enormous broad canvas behind and little intimate scenes happening in front, but scenes of great importance. I just find these plays much bigger than *Juno* and *Shadow*; each one has taken on a depth of style. I don't think it's very difficult to see the step from *The Plough* to *The Silver Tassie*, the step from *The Silver Tassie* to *Within the Gates*. Later on his style changed again, and he married song, dance and drama all together in his more abstract plays, such as *Cock-a-Doodle Dandy* and *Figuro in the Night*.

Did Sean see much theatre once your family moved to Devon?
No, not a lot. When he was very young, of course, he went to see a lot of the music halls and he went to see touring companies. He did see Henry Irving, and he told me that Irving had real grass with rabbits running round, and that the plays were cut to suit him. He also saw touring opera companies as well as touring theatre companies; Dion Boucicault of course and then, when the Abbey started, he saw Shaw and Synge, Ibsen and Strindberg – all those. One mustn't forget that in those days that the Abbey wasn't quite what *we* think of the Abbey. Yeats's ideas for his sets and costumes were quite extraordinary really. Sean described to me one of Robert Gregory's sets for a W. B. Yeats play which was very symbolic. He just had a golden mast and a green sail and that was it. I think Yeats and Lady Gregory were in contact with Edward Gordon Craig, the great designer and, as far as I know, they had a set that either was suggested by him or designed by him, of flats that could be used for almost every play. When Sean went to London, he saw the Habima Players. They were from Moscow and they were expressionistic. They did *The Dybbuk* and *A Midsummer Night's Dream* with amazing sets and costumes. Marc Chagall designed for them in Moscow; they even used to make up their faces in a stylized way. Sean saw that, and took off.

Did you use masks for Behind the Green Curtains?
I did want to put some of the characters in masks, but they weren't ready for it, so we used stylized make-up instead. I had worked with John Blatchley on the mask – the half-mask, or comic mask, and the full mask, or tragic mask – incorporating animal improvization and 'characteristics'. I have always been fascinated by the power of the mask.

It's important to understand the style of Sean's work. I saw a production of *Cock-a-Doodle Dandy*, done at the Royal Court in 1959, and Sean Kenny did the sets and the costumes for that. I think he's a very good designer, but neither Sean or I thought it was right. A great big ungainly cockerel, you know, when it's supposed to be this life force; and the cottage was like a little Irish cottage – it was an incorrect concept. I know it isn't easy but I think it's fundamental to be honest to the text. The main thing is the play, and the understanding of the play, its style, its rhythm, its theme and its objective – what it tells you and how it tells you it. You have to cast it well, as without the right actors a play can't live. On top of that you have to have a director, designer, composer, lighting designer, and above all this there is imagination. It's an exciting challenge.

Could you talk about the one-man show you did with Niall Buggy?
Song at Sunset is the story of Sean's life told through his writings: extracts from his plays, letters and autobiographies. I compiled the piece to tell the story of the man I knew. I worked closely with the actor Niall Buggy, who played Sean and all the other characters – well over twenty of them. We started the project at the Hampstead Theatre. I also used audio tapes Sean made in the last years of his life. These are in colloquial speech, and so I used as much from them as possible. Parts of them are similar to the autobiographies. On these tapes he decided to sing all the songs in the autobiographies, but then he talks around them, telling stories, some similar to those in the auto- biographies, but he tells them in a different way, in a more

colloquial style. I tried to make it mainly him, his words and writing. I wrote very little of it myself. I think it would go very well as a double bill with the documentary I'm making about him. The one-man show tells his life absolutely from beginning to end and the documentary is a personal account of the man, from his wife and two surviving children, with extracts from two television interviews he gave and from some of his plays. I think together they could be a useful educational tool for students.

Having worked on many of the later plays, do you feel that they might provide more scope for younger people or students than the Dublin Trilogy?
Possibly, although it depends how you are teaching your students. Sometimes it's better for students to start with a more 'realistic' play, then later they may be able to add 'style' to their work, exaggerate themselves physically in a truthful way. *Purple Dust* would be a very good play for students to do and it's also dramatic, funny. You could use costumes to exaggerate the characters and clown around in rehearsal more than you finally would, to stretch the imagination. Sometimes you find that, when young people go out dancing, they do all these amazing things with their bodies and then you put them up onstage and they become stiff and awkward. So to work with a relaxed body and voice is a very important thing for students to get to. And *The Drums of Father Ned* is fun to do. I saw a production with lots of young people that David Phethean did at Hornchurch; most of them were much too young for the old parts, but it worked very well. And then there's *Hall of Healing* and the earlier one-act plays – or even just to do the pub scene from *Plough*, which was originally a one-act play called *The Cooing of the Doves*. The important thing is to try to stretch the imagination and relax into character.

How did Sean feel about the productions of his own work that he saw?
He was pretty pragmatic about them. I was around when he

sat in on rehearsals for a production of *Purple Dust*. Sam Wanamaker, the director, introduced a lot of extra songs. Sean thought there were too many, but he was pretty nice about it, let Sam include most of them. He had a pretty clear idea of what he wanted to see in his plays, and I think if he saw a production and it wasn't quite right, he'd say, 'Maybe next time.' With the production of *Within the Gates* in New York in 1934, he rewrote it quite considerably during rehearsals. If you read the original version that was done in London before the New York one, it's quite different. There are some of his last plays that he never saw; he was almost blind by then. He never saw *The Bishop's Bonfire*, and he never saw *The Drums of Father Ned*, *Behind the Green Curtains* or *Figuro in the Night*. I don't know how many other playwrights that's happened to. But he relied on Eileen to be his eyes. Yes, it must have been quite strange. I suppose someone could have recorded the plays that were put on and sent the recordings to him, but no one thought of that in those days.

My brother Breon did some designs for productions, but they were never used. He and Sean used to talk a lot together about painting. Sean would like to have been a painter – that was what he wanted to be rather than a writer – but he couldn't afford all the equipment. All the letters I had from him had lovely funny drawings. He loved to draw; he designed the covers to the early editions of his work, and another artist adapted them. They didn't actually look as nice as the originals, but he designed them – he liked doing that. He had a natural eye for good work, and he loved colour. For instance, once, when he was a young man, he was looking in the window of one of those religious shops in Dublin, and he saw a Madonna and Child and said, 'That's really beautiful,' and among the rest he had actually picked out one that was by – I don't know – a real painter, say, Tintoretto. The second-hand books he bought then weren't all to do with literature; he bought a lot of art books, Fra Angelico and Raphael. A lot of the old books weren't coloured, but he was very interested in them all the same. So I think that's why his plays have it all in them, they're so visual. And the music as well: he wasn't so educated about that, but he had a love for music. He believed in all these elements coming together in drama, like they do in *Cock-a-Doodle Dandy*, and his later plays.

What did Sean think about you going into theatre?
I think, if I'd done anything artistically, he'd have wanted me to paint, or be a scenic designer. But that's just as precarious as acting. I think he'd have been very pleased if I'd been a biologist or something!

Bibliography

Editions of O'Casey's Plays

Sean O'Casey: Plays 1, London: Faber and Faber, 1998
  (includes *Juno and the Paycock*, *Within the Gates*, *Red
  Roses for Me*, *Cock-a-Doodle Dandy*)
Sean O'Casey: Plays 2, London: Faber and Faber, 1998
  (includes *The Shadow of a Gunman*, *The Plough and the
  Stars*, *The Silver Tassie*, *Purple Dust*, *Hall of Healing*)
Three Dublin Plays, London: Faber and Faber, 1998 (includes
  The Shadow of a Gunman, *Juno and the Paycock*, *The
  Plough and the Stars*)

Editions of O'Casey's Other Writings

Autobiographies I, London: Papermac, 1992 (includes *I
  Knock at the Door*, *Pictures in the Hallway*, *Drums Under
  the Window*)
Autobiographies II, London: Papermac, 1992 (includes
  Inishfallen, Fare Thee Well, *Rose and Crown*, *Sunset and
  Evening Star*)
Windfalls: Stories and Poems, London: Macmillan, 1934
  (includes the short plays *The End of the Beginning* and *A
  Pound on Demand*)
The Green Crow, New York: Braziller, 1956 (includes short
  stories, and essays on theatre)
Under a Colored Cap, London: Macmillan, 1963 (includes
  various essays on culture and religion, and a riposte to the
  criticisms levelled at *Purple Dust*)
Feathers from a Green Crow: Sean O'Casey 1905–1925 ed.
  Robert Hogan, London: Macmillan, 1963 (includes 'The
  Sacrifice of Thomas Ashe' and 'The Story of the Irish
  Citizen Army')

Blasts and Benedictions: Articles and Stories, selected and
  introduced by Ronald Ayling, London: Macmillan, 1967
  (includes O'Casey's response to Yeats's criticisms of *The
  Silver Tassie*, and the essays 'The Bald Primaqueera' and
  'Not Waiting for Godot')
The Letters of Sean O'Casey Volume I: 1910–1941, edited by
  David Krause, New York: Macmillan, 1975
The Letters of Sean O'Casey Volume II: 1942–1954, edited
  by David Krause, New York: Macmillan, 1975
The Letters of Sean O'Casey Volume III: 1955–1958, edited
  by David Krause, Washington: Catholic University Press of
  America, 1989
The Letters of Sean O'Casey Volume IV: 1959–1964, edited
  by David Krause, Washington: Catholic University Press of
  America, 1992

Critical Works on O'Casey
Ayling, Ronald, ed., *Sean O'Casey: Modern Judgements*,
  London: Macmillan, 1969 (a variety of pieces, including
  Yeats's letter rejecting *The Silver Tassie* and some early
  critical appreciations)
– *O'Casey: The Dublin Trilogy*, London: Macmillan, 1985
  (includes reviews and accounts of the first productions of
  these plays, as well as contemporary critical essays)
– and Michael Durcan, *Sean O'Casey: A Bibliography*
  London: Macmillan, 1978
Doherty, Francis, 'Displacing the Hero in Modern Irish
  Drama', *Theatre Research International* 15.1 (1990) 41–55
  (this compares the concept of the hero in works by Synge,
  O'Casey and Beckett)
Fallon, Gabriel, *Sean O'Casey: The Man I Knew*, London:
  Routledge & Kegan Paul, 1965 (a memoir by a friend of
  O'Casey who was closely associated with the Abbey
  Theatre as both an actor and board member)
Grene, Nicolas, *The Politics of Irish Drama: From Boucicault
  to Friel*, Cambridge: Cambridge University Press, 1999

(includes a chapter on the relationship between class and
space in O'Casey's plays)

Hunt, Hugh, *Sean O'Casey*, Dublin: Gill and Macmillan,
1980 (a brief biographical study)

Innes, Christopher, 'The Essential Continuity of Sean
O'Casey', *Modern Drama* 33.3 (1990) pp. 419–33 (an arti-
cle which traces continuities of style and theme throughout
O'Casey's career)

Jones, Nesta, *File on O'Casey* London: Methuen, 1986 (a
valuable reference guide with synopses and performance
histories as well as biographical information)

Kilroy, Thomas, *Sean O'Casey: A Collection of Critical
Essays*, London: Prentice Hall, 1975

Krause, David, *Sean O'Casey: The Man and his Work*,
London: MacGibbon & Kee, 1960 (this study combines
biography with critical assessment and makes a good starting point for further reading)

— and Robert G. Lowery, eds., *Sean O'Casey: Centenary
Essays*, Gerrards Cross: Colin Smythe, 1980

Lowery, Robert G., *A Whirlwind in Dublin: The Plough and
the Stars Riots*, Westport, Conn.: Greenwood Press, 1984

Maxwell, D. E. S., *A Critical History of Modern Irish Drama
1891–1980*, Cambridge: Cambridge University Press, 1984
(as well as tracing the early development of the Abbey, this
includes a chapter on O'Casey which examines his use of
language and his representation of women)

Mikhail, E. K., *Sean O'Casey: A Bibliography of Criticism*,
London: Macmillan, 1972

Murray, Christopher, *Twentieth-Century Irish Drama: Mirror
up to a Nation*, Manchester: Manchester University Press,
1997 (this study includes a chapter dealing with O'Casey's
notion of the hero)

— *Sean O'Casey*, London: Faber and Faber, 2000 (a concise
and useful study focusing on the Dublin plays and considering historical context and issues relating to the plays in
performance)

O'Casey, Eileen, *Sean*, London: Pan Books, 1973 (a memoir of her husband written by Sean O'Casey's widow)

Schrank, Bernice, *Sean O'Casey: A Research and Production Sourcebook*, Westport, Conn.: Greenwood Press, 1996 (a valuable guide to productions of the plays and for locating further reading)

Thomson, Leslie, 'Opening the Eyes of the Audience: Visual and Verbal Imagery in *Juno and the Paycock*', *Modern Drama* 29.4 (1986) 556–66 (this article focuses on the relationship between Johnny and Juno as the centre of the play)

Watt, Stephen, *Joyce, O'Casey and the Irish Popular Theatre*, New York: Syracuse University Press, 1991 (includes a chapter on the influence of melodrama on O'Casey's writing)

Welch, Robert, ed., *The Oxford Companion to Irish Literature*, Oxford: Clarendon Press, 1996 (a useful reference source on all aspects of Irish writing)

Acknowledgements

I would like to thank all those who generously agreed to be interviewed for this book and who took the time to comment on drafts and respond to queries. Their contributions have been invaluable. The staffs of St Matthias Library, UWE, The Theatre Collection, University of Bristol and the British Library Colindale also gave a great deal of assistance.

Thanks also to those who gave help, support and advice throughout the development of this project: Richard Boon, Vicky Dunne, Scott Fraser, Nick Freeman, Bill Greenslade, Elizabeth Hazlehurst, Robin Jarvis, Phil Ollerenshaw, Peggy Paterson and Amanda Salter.

For permission to reprint copyright material the publishers gratefully acknowledge the following:

B. CROWTHER: 'Who is Then the Gentleman?' first published in the *New York Times*, 14 October 1934 © *New York Times* 1934; reproduced with permission of The *New York Times* Agency; B. ATKINSON: 'Critic at Large: Visit with Sean O'Casey' first published in the *New York Times*, 31 December 1934 © *New York Times* 1934: reprinted with the permission of The *New York Times* Agency; W. J. WETHERBY: 'The Figure In the Shadows', extract from *Guardian* 10 September 1959 © *Guardian* 1959 'The Sting and the Twinkle', extract from *Guardian*, 15 August 1962 © *Guardian* 1962; SEAN O'CASEY: 'Last Thoughts from O'Casey' first published 20 September 1964 © *Telegraph* Group Limited, 1964; LESLIE REES: 'Remembrance of Things Past II: On Meeting Sean O'Casey', originally published in *Meanjin Quarterly*, Melbourne,

Australia, December 1964; UNSIGNED: 'Echoes of the Town' first published in the *Daily Sketch*, reproduced with the permission of *Daily Sketch*/Associated Newspapers; 'O'Casey Explains Himself', first printed in the *Daily Sketch*, reproduced with permission of *Daily Sketch*/Associated Newspapers, 'The Rebel Who Never Retired' first published in the *News Chronicle*, reproduced with permission of *News Chronicle*/Associated Newspapers.

Faber and Faber apologize for any errors or omissions in the above list and would be grateful to be notified of any corrections that should be incorporated in the next edition or reprint of this volume

Index